Folens

Book

3

LANGUAGE WORKS

Contents

Term 1: Part 1		Page
Read the Story	The Elephant Chase	4
Exercises		5
Grammar	Ending the Word with **a**, **i**, **o** and **u**	6
Creative Writing	Opening Sentences	7
Read the Story	Eagles – Kings of the Birds	8
Exercises		9
Grammar	Direct Speech	10
Grammar	Prefix Meanings	11
Grammar	Capital Letters	12
Creative Writing	Paragraphs	13
Poetry	'We Won't Tell You Again!'	14
Grammar	Word Roots	15
Read the Story	Jo's Gift	16
Exercises		17
Grammar	Nouns	18
Grammar	Using a Thesaurus	19

Term 1: Part 2		Page
Read the Story	The Loch Ness Monster	20
Exercises		21
Grammar	Verbs 1	22
Grammar	Verbs 2	23
Grammar	Choosing the Best Adverb	24
Creative Writing	Book Reviews	25
Read the Story	The Lion, the Witch and the Wardrobe	26
Exercises		27
Grammar	Indirect Speech	28
Grammar	Adjectives	29
Grammar	Standard English 1	30
Grammar	Idioms and Clichés	31
Read the Story	Marie Curie	32
Exercises		33
Grammar	Singular or Plural	34
Grammar	Standard English 2	35
Poetry	Questions at Night	36
Creative Writing	Use Your Imagination	37

Term 2: Part 1		Page
Read the Story	Wuthering Heights	38
Exercises		39
Grammar	Sentence Contractions	40
Creative Writing	What Happened Next?	41
Read the Story	The Space Shuttle	42
Exercises		43
Grammar	Where Do the Commas Go?	44
Grammar	Adverbs	45
Creative Writing	Action Paragraphs	46
Grammar	Spelling Rules	47
Read the Story	The Sheep-Pig	48
Exercises		49
Grammar	Homophones	50
Phonics	Soft **c**	51
Phonics	Letter Strings	52
Grammar	Possessive Pronouns	53

Term 2: Part 2		Page
Read the Story	Natural Disasters	54
Exercises		55
Grammar	Asking Questions/Compound Words	56
Phonics	Suffixes – **sion**, **tion** and **cian**	57
Creative Writing	Finish the Story/Meeting a New Face	58
Grammar	Words Often Confused	59
Read the Story	Little House on the Prairie	60
Exercises		61
Grammar	Antonyms	62
Creative Writing	Descriptions	63
Creative Writing	Onomatopoeia	64
Grammar	Figures of Speech	65
Grammar	Changing Sentences	66
Grammar	In Agreement	67
Creative Writing	Interesting Sentences	68
Poetry	Country Cat	69

Term 3: Part 1		Page
Read the Story	Bigfoot	70
Exercises		71
Grammar	The Apostrophe – Possessive Nouns	72
Grammar	Using a Dictionary	73
Grammar	Changing Words	74
Grammar	Dropping and Keeping **e**	75
Read the Story	Midwinter Day	76
Exercises		77
Grammar	Prepositions	78
Creative Writing	Interviews	79
Creative Writing	A–Z Factfile/What Happened Next?	80
Oral Language	Cleaning Up	81

Term 3: Part 2		Page
Read the Story	Where Eagles Dare	82
Exercises		83
Poetry	Dahn the Plug'ole	84
Oral Language	Timber!	85
Grammar	The **y** Rule	86
Grammar	Proof-reading	87
Grammar	Prefixes – Spellings and Meanings	88
Oral Language	Air Disaster	89
Poetry	A Wanderer's Song	90
Grammar	Many Languages	91
Oral Language	Donkey Rides	92
Oral Language	In for the High Jump	93
Grammar	The **i**, **e** and **c** Rule	94
Creative Writing	Write a Letter/Questionnaires	95
Oral Language	Sitting Around	96

The Elephant Chase

In The Great Elephant Chase, *Tad Hawkins, a fifteen-year-old orphan boy, meets Cissie, a seemingly crippled young girl and an elephant named 'Khush'. From that moment on, their lives become entwined in a dramatic journey across America.*

There was a gasp, a buzz of whispers – and then a fearful, petrified silence. Everyone in the crowd gazed up at the unconscious girl in the elephant's trunk.

I should have done something, Tad thought. He stared up at the elephant, but its face was blank. Incomprehensible. Everyone was waiting for the showman to speak, but he was staring as hard as anyone else.

It was the girl's mother who broke the silence. "Get her down." The whisper was more terrifying than a scream. "She has a weak heart. *Get her down.*"

Mrs Bobb gasped and there was a murmur of sympathy. The showman stepped forward. He raised his voice, speaking to the whole crowd. "*Complete* silence, if you please."

It came, uncannily fast. For a hundred yards, on each side, the tracks were lined with silent people. There was nothing to be heard except the grinding of the coal-breakers, away on Horsehead Mountain.

The showman took a step back and waved his stick at the elephant, its little steel tip glinting in the morning sunlight. "Khush. Down," he commanded. The elephant's eyes flickered, but it did not move. The man rapped the stick on the ground and spoke more sharply. "Khush. No."

For an instant, no one breathed and Tad's chest was tight with fear. Then, very slowly, the thick trunk began to uncurl. The elephant lowered the girl towards the ground and the showman took her into his arms, with her head flopped back and her eyes closed.

"Is she – dead?" The young woman stretched out a shaking arm.

"Not dead, ma'am." The showman's voice carried over the crowd. "The shock to her nervous system has put her into a catalepsy. But I can cure that, if you will allow me."

"You will let him touch her?" Mrs Bobb muttered.

"Anything!" The mother clutched at the showman's arm. "*Anything* that will bring her to herself!"

He smiled down at her. "Could I trouble you to fetch my bag from the depot?"

The showman pulled out a small, corked bottle made of clear glass, lifted it high in the air, so that everyone saw. Kneeling down, the showman laid the unconscious girl across his lap and took a little silver spoon from his pocket.

Slowly, giving everyone round him the chance to observe, he tipped the green liquid into the girl's mouth.

Gillian Cross

A **Answer these questions.**

1. Why do you think the 'buzz of whispers' became a 'petrified silence'?
2. Why do you think Tad felt that he should have done something?
3. Why was the girl's mother so worried?
4. Which sentence indicates that the showman wanted everybody to hear his conversation with the mother?
5. How did the crowd respond to the showman? Why?
6. What do you think the showman meant when he said, "The shock to her nervous system has put her into a catalepsy"?
7. What do you think the green liquid will do to the girl?
8. Give the passage a new title of your own.

 B **Match the words to their meanings.**

Use your dictionary, if necessary, to match the words on the left with their correct meanings. Then write them in suitable sentences.

unconscious	impossible to understand
uncannily	gleaming, flashing
petrified	to notice, to watch
glinting	not aware, with no feeling
incomprehensible	paralysed with fear
observe	strangely, mysteriously

 C **Reread the passage.**

The elephant has a character of its own in this passage.

1. Write down four phrases that tell you about the elephant.
2. In your own words, write down what the elephant does in the story.
3. Write a paragraph describing the elephant. Say what you think its attitude to the girl is.

 D **Imagine you are the little girl.**

How did you feel when you woke up? What do you remember? Write some sentences about it. Remember to use the first person 'I'.

Ending the Word with **a, i, o** and **u**

When a word ends in **o** we usually add **s** or **es** to make the plural.

piano ⟶ pianos   but   potato ⟶ potatoes

 Write down the plurals for these words.

memo

tomato

echo

photo

casino

mango

Check the meaning of words you do not know in a dictionary.

Some words ending in **a, i, o** and **u** do not change when we write them as plurals.

 Decide what the plurals of these words are and write them down.

haiku

gnu

cocoa

taxi

umbrella

Find out what language they come from.

 What language do you think this word comes from?

plateau

1. Check the meaning of it in a dictionary.
2. Find out what letter we add to make it plural.
3. Write a sentence for it in the plural.

Opening Sentences

- The pictures below are all taken from a story about incidents on a cruise liner. The author has already prepared one exciting incident which happens near the beginning of the story when a man falls overboard and nearly drowns.

- When writing a complete story, you first need to think about capturing the reader's interest, right from the beginning.

- A good opening will do this by:

    a. describing the scene of the story

    b. amusing the readers

    c. starting with somebody saying something dramatic or unusual.

 Look at these openings and answer the questions that follow.

1. As the prince walked serenely on board, his accompanying bodyguard stumbled over a suitcase and somersaulted over his unsuspecting master.

2. "Help! I'm drowning. Can't swim," the huge bodyguard gasped, before sinking with hands flailing about.

3. The gigantic, majestic ocean liner cruised through the choppy wild sea, like a juggernaut steaming down the highway.

1. Write a sentence which describes the cruise liner waiting at the dock for its passengers.

2. Who was the prince and why was he joining the cruise?

3. Write a few sentences to link pictures **1** and **2**. Describe the bodyguard falling into the sea, making it funny if you can.

4. How was the bodyguard saved from drowning? Describe how he was rescued and brought back on board.

5. Now describe the other passengers and the liner setting sail. Finish your episode with the lines from picture **3**.

Eagles – Kings of the Birds

The eagles are the most majestic and impressive **(1)** in the world. Armed with sharp talons and curved beaks, eagles are able to tackle a wide variety of prey, mostly small mammals. Plunging down from on high, the eagles seize their **(2)** in their clawed feet and carry them away to some isolated crag before eating them. The name eagle is given to very different birds in different countries. Some are small, others large, but they all share the features of being active hunting birds with the female being larger than the male.

Generally considered to be the most impressive is the golden eagle, which may be found in remote areas throughout much of the northern hemisphere. It frequents **(3)** areas where it can be safe from human interference. It hunts by patrolling the skies on its 6 foot (1.8 metres) wide wings, scanning the ground below for a potential victim. Lifting on thermals and updraughts, the eagle may rise to a height of 300 feet (90 metres) or more. When the eagle sees a movement, it may turn out of the thermal to investigate. Gradually losing height as it approaches the site of the disturbance, it watches the ground intently.

When a rodent or small bird is spotted, the eagle partially folds its wings and drops from the sky at speeds approaching 100 miles (161 kilometres) per hour. Landing on the prey with a powerful impact, the eagle pins it to the ground before flying off with it. Surprise is essential, for the eagle hunts rodents and rabbits which are themselves fast movers and can dive into a burrow in **(4)**.

When hunting, the crested serpent eagle abandons the high-level cruising of its fellow eagles. Instead it sits almost motionless on a convenient branch or rock, sweeping the ground ceaselessly with its eyes. When a snake slides across the ground, it is detected by the eagle which watches its progress. If the snake moves off, the bird loses interest, but if it comes close to the eagle's perch, the bird leaps into action. Taking briefly to the wing, the eagle **(5)** vertically down to the snake, which is lifted clear off the ground and carried to the perch.

Golden eagles have been blamed for carrying off human babies left momentarily unguarded and several apparently reliable reports of this exist. Many are sceptical of these reports, but an eagle can carry a weight of around 15 pounds (7 kilograms) so a new-born baby would be within its prey range.

From *Birds of the World*, produced by Ted Smart
(author Rupert O. Matthews)

A **Write the most suitable word for each number in the passage, from the lines below.**

1. insects	cars	birds	creatures
2. young	victims	enemies	flowers
3. mountainous	busy	arctic	dreary
4. days	hours	seconds	minutes
5. jumps	scans	somersaults	drops

 B **Answer these questions.**

1. What is the most common prey that eagles attack?

2. How do they catch their prey?

3. What do we learn about the female?

4. Why would you not normally expect to see an eagle in a town or city?

5. Explain in your own words how the eagle captures its prey.

6. What do you think 'thermals' and 'updraughts' are?

7. Why do you think the eagle partially folds its wings before diving from the sky?

8. Why do you think poisonous snakes are unable to bite an eagle while they are being carried?

9. Is it cruel that eagles live by eating smaller creatures? How do you feel about it?

10. What problems might there be in having a pet eagle?

 C **Each numbered sentence tells us something that happens (the effect). In each group, choose the sentence which explains why or gives a reason (the cause).**

1. Eagles can easily seize their victims *because*

   a. the victims surrender.

   b. eagles are the fastest birds.

   c. eagles are armed with sharp talons and curved beaks.

2. When hunting, eagles may first rise to a height of 300 feet *because*

   a. they enjoy riding on the thermals and updraughts.

   b. they cannot be seen by their victims.

   c. they think better at that height.

 D **Write single sentences explaining what each paragraph is generally about, like this.**

The first paragraph tells us how eagles catch their prey, that there are different kinds of eagles and what they have in common.

Direct Speech

"Who's that?" Ramish whispered to Karen.

"That is Mr Giacomi," replied Karen. "He is a very great artiste of the trampoline."

- Notice that only the words actually spoken (i.e. direct speech) are enclosed by speech marks. Notice also that the question mark, comma and full stop are always placed inside the speech marks.

 Show the correct use of speech marks in the pictures. (Write full sentences, indicating the speaker.)

 Rewrite these sentences inserting speech marks, capital letters, commas, question marks and full stops.

1. the ringmaster declared let the show begin
2. i've a terrible toothache moaned sanjit
3. don't shoot pleaded the bank robber i'm coming out with my hands up
4. i sentence you to five years hard labour said the judge have you anything to say for yourself
5. why don't we have a midnight feast asked natalie
6. indiana jones announced i have found the lost ark
7. why didn't you catch me complained young giacomi to his brother
8. did you eat anything strange asked the doctor

- Look at the positioning of the spoken lines on page 4. Notice that when the speaker changes, a new paragraph begins. This is an important rule of the writing of dialogue between people.

 Rewrite the following correctly.

it was long after midnight when josie finally arrived at the feast what kept you you're over an hour late jean shouted out to her i'm sorry said josie i'm afraid i slept in better late than never said jean i hope you brought those chocolate biscuits with you josie

Prefix Meanings

 A **Read the meanings of these words.**

autocrat	a person who rules completely, by him/herself
automatic	moving or happening by itself, of its own accord
bicentenary	two-hundredth anniversary
bicuspid	teeth with two fangs or points
circumnavigate	to sail round something
circumlocution	a wordy or roundabout way of speaking
telescope	an instrument for making far-away objects look near
televise	to send information by television
transmit	to send from one place or person to another
transatlantic	crossing the Atlantic

 B **Split the words into their syllables and write them out. Underline the prefix in each word. This will help you remember the spelling.**

Decide what the prefixes mean and write them out.

 C **Try to work out the meanings of these words and then check them in a dictionary.**

autobiography   circumference   telecommunications   transplant

 D **Write a question for each one to show its meaning.**

Don't forget the question mark.

Capital Letters

Use capital letters:
1. At the start of every sentence.
2. When naming days, months and festivals.
3. When writing the pronoun 'I'.
4. When naming particular people, places and languages.

 A **Rewrite the passage correctly.**

the ship had set sail two days before christmas, on wednesday the 23rd of december. the helicopter hovered over the survivors. their prayers had been answered. mary stewart from new york was saved from drowning by a journalist visiting from germany, who spoke excellent english. when i heard about the rescue, i was very relieved.

Use capital letters also:
5. When writing the first word of a direct quotation.
6. When referring to a person's title, e.g. Ms Kelly.
7. In initials and some abbreviations.
8. For the first word and all important words in titles of books, films, poems, newspapers, etc.
9. For the first word in a new line of some poetry.

 B **Rewrite this passage, inserting capital letters in the appropriate places. End each sentence by putting in the correct punctuation mark.**

a hush ran round the packed dining-room as the groom rose to speak he looked nervously at his mischievous friend johnny b. looney then he took a deep breath and stuttered fitfully, "today, saturday the 7th of july, is a day i've dreamed about for a long ..."

at this stage, dr baggio from italy, who had taken up residence in the area, burst through the doors and announced his apologies in very broken english he muttered something about thinking it was friday then he feverishly inquired, "have i missed anything"

as the room erupted in comic uproar, johnny voiced the opinion that dr baggio must have been watching 'friday the 13th' the groom collapsed into his chair

Paragraphs

- A paragraph is a collection of related sentences which focus on one main idea. Sometimes one particular sentence will describe the main idea. It is called the topic sentence. All the rest of the sentences which help to describe the main idea are called supporting details.

 Copy the topic sentence in the next two paragraphs.

1. It was quite by chance that Stone Age people discovered how to start a fire. Perhaps someone was trying to sharpen a tool by striking flint off it. It must have surprised them when they saw sparks jump and ignite dry leaves or twigs. Or maybe two pieces of wood were rubbed together, until the constant rubbing caused dry leaves to be kindled by the hot dust produced. The discoverer of this method may just have been passing time.

2. Fire kept the Stone Age people warm, especially at night. When darkness fell, the fire provided light and may have scared off wild prowling animals, thus protecting families. They used fire for cooking, especially when roasting meat. Fire brought people together and communication and storytelling began. Without doubt, fire became a great friend to the Stone Age people.

 Read this paragraph and pick out the main idea from the three options below.

Tyrannosaurus was the largest known flesh-eating animal which has ever lived on land. It was 12 metres long, 5 metres high and weighed around 7 tonnes. Its teeth were 15 centimetres long and each one had saw-edges like steak knives for tearing meat. Tyrannosaurus had very powerful hind legs and huge clawed feet to grip and tear its prey. The front legs or 'arms' were tiny and the hands had only two fingers. They seem to have been almost useless for they could not even reach the mouth.

Which is the main idea?

The size of Tyrannosaurus' mouth.
What Tyrannosaurus looked like.
Why Tyrannosaurus had short front legs.

 Now write a short paragraph about your favourite animal.

Don't forget to use one main idea.

'We Won't Tell You Again!'

It makes me sullen and wilful and wild
The way I'm described as a difficult child.
They shake their heads wherever I go
And tell each other, "I told you so."
They tell each other and even a friend,
"We don't quite know where it all will end."
And tale on tale they have mournfully piled
On the life they lead with a difficult child.

But when I'm sweet and I smile and purr,
They say to each other, "Now what's with her?"
And when I'm cuddly and kind and warm,
They say it's the calm before the storm.
And when I offer a hug or kiss
They're murmuring, "What are you up to, Miss?"

Max Fatchen

A **Answer these questions.**

1. What is meant by the phrase 'a difficult child'? Which other words mean the same?
2. Explain in your own words how the girl feels when she is described in this way.
3. To whom is the poet referring with the words 'They shake their heads ...'?
4. Which words in the poem tell you how 'they' feel when relating tales to their friends?
5. Are 'they' pleased when the girl is sweet? Which words might describe their reaction?
6. What does the phrase 'calm before the storm' mean? Think of your own saying to describe a child who is sulky.
7. Has anybody ever asked you what you were up to?
   Describe and illustrate what you were doing.
8. Write and illustrate three different 'tales' that might describe the girl's difficult behaviour.

B **Write a poem describing how you feel when people describe you in a certain way.**

Begin with the words 'It makes me ... '

Word Roots

 A **Write the following words in five groups.**
Then underline the root word for each group.

bombard	signature	permission	sign	bomb	permit

sand	dead	deadline	signal	bombshell	sandpaper

B **Now write down the meaning of each root word.**

Check any words you don't know in a dictionary.

C **Write down the roots of these words.**

journalist   rooster

D **Use a dictionary to find words which come from these root words.**

bound   break   globe

E **Write down the letter patterns for these groups of words.**

Example: home women = ome

1. permit   remit   admit
2. escape   scapegoat   landscape
3. cab   cabinet   cabin
4. riddance   ridden   riddle

Jo's Gift

Little Women is the story of four young women growing up in America during the time of the Civil War.

The short afternoon wore away; all the other errands were done, and Meg and her mother were busy at some necessary needle-work, while Beth and Amy got tea, and Hannah finished her ironing with what she called a 'slap and a bang', but still Jo did not come. They began to get anxious; and Laurie went off to find her, for no one ever knew what freak Jo might take into her head. He missed her, however, and she came walking in with a very queer expression of countenance, for there was a mixture of fun and fear, satisfaction and regret in it, which puzzled the family as much as did the roll of bills she laid before her mother, saying, with a little choke in her voice, "That's my contribution towards making father comfortable and bringing him home!"

"My dear, where did you get it? Twenty-five dollars! Jo, I hope you haven't done anything rash?"

"No, it's mine honestly; I didn't beg, borrow, nor steal it. I earned it; and I don't think you'll blame me, for I only sold what was my own."

As she spoke, Jo took off her bonnet, and a general outcry arose, for all her abundant hair was cut short.

"Your hair! Your beautiful hair!" "Oh, Jo, how could you? Your one beauty." "My dear girl, there was no need of this." "She don't look like my Jo any more, but I love her dearly for it!"

As everyone exclaimed, and Beth hugged the cropped head tenderly, Jo assumed an indifferent air, which did not deceive any one a particle, and said, rumpling up the brown bush, and trying to look as if she liked it, "It doesn't affect the fate of the nation, so don't wail, Beth. It will be good for my vanity; I was getting too proud of my wig. It will do my brains good to have that mop taken off; my head feels deliciously light and cool, and the barber said I could soon have a curly crop, which will be boyish, becoming, and easy to keep in order. I'm satisfied; so please take the money, and let's have supper."

"Tell me all about it, Jo; *I* am not quite satisfied, but I can't blame you, for I know how willingly you sacrificed your vanity, as you call it, to your love. But, my dear, it was not necessary, and I'm afraid you will regret it, one of these days," said Mrs March.

"No I won't!" returned Jo, stoutly, feeling much relieved that her prank was not entirely condemned.

From *Little Women* by Louisa May Alcott

A **Check the meaning of these words in a dictionary.**

abundant   vanity   contribution   condemn

 B **Pick the word from the list that means the same as the bold word.**

1. anxious	obsolete	arise	arrange	nervous
2. errand	estate	task	respect	error
3. honest	truthful	desire	frighten	respectful
4. indifferent	careless	increase	unconcerned	independent
5. relief	relish	ease	connect	linger
6. absurd	silly	wise	atone	accent

 C **Answer these questions.**

1. What do you think Hannah means by doing the ironing with a 'slap and a bang'?
2. How can you tell the family didn't have much money?
3. What did they need extra money for?
4. What was Jo's 'one beauty'?
5. How do you think Jo really felt about her short hair? How can you tell?
6. How did Mrs March feel about what Jo had done?
7. Write three sentences which describe Jo's personality.

 D **Read the first sentence again.**

Think about what is happening. Why are the last six words important? Why do you think the writer has put them at the end?

 E **Read the whole opening paragraph again.**

1. Think of two other ways the passage could have begun and write down your ideas.
2. Choose one and write three opening sentences.

17

Nouns

- A noun is the name of a person, place, creature or thing. Common nouns begin with lower-case letters as they name general things – horse, doctor, building, girl, city.
- Proper nouns begin with capital letters as they name something particular – Arkle, Dr Baggio, Leicester Square, Louise, Las Vegas.

 Write out the common and proper nouns in these sentences.

1. Michelle has won a fantastic Christmas holiday for her family.
2. Their exciting destination was Paris, France.
3. Finally, 24 December arrived and the snow was falling gently from the sky.
4. The family boarded the 'World Airways' plane and Michelle strapped her seat belt on.
5. The pilot, Leanne Marsh, announced that the journey would take two hours.
6. During the pleasant trip the passengers saw the English Channel and parts of Brittany.
7. At the airport, a little boy, whose name was Peter, was crying because he'd lost his parents.
8. Fortunately, a police officer named Jacques Papin recovered the lost child.

B **Rewrite this passage. Add suitable nouns to fill in the blanks.**

When the hippopotamus opened its ugly _____ , it displayed two massive, sharp _____ protruding from its lower _____ . That was enough to send _____ down my spine!

Then a giraffe stretched its long _____ and stole a juicy _____ that I was about to eat, right out of my _____ .

As I stared in disbelief, an African _____ , complete with two ivory _____ , bellowed loudly in my _____ . Seconds later, I was drenched to the _____ .

Using A Thesaurus

- When we want to find a word that has a similar meaning to another (a synonym) we can use a thesaurus. This is organised in alphabetical order, like a dictionary.

- For example, I want to find a synonym for the word shy. I look under 's' in my thesaurus and find this:

  shy *adjective*
  Alternative words: timid, bashful, self-conscious, introverted

- Which word will I choose? It depends on what I am writing about.

  Rover was sitting quietly in the corner and would not come when he was called; he seemed such a timid creature.

  "Lena was a very talented musician, but always worried about her performance, so I suppose you would say she was an introverted person," said Anne.

 Find synonyms for these words and write them down.

tragic   licence   harm   drip

 Choose two synonyms for each word.

Write sentences to show their meanings. (You will need to write eight sentences.)

- We can also use a thesaurus to find a word that is opposite in meaning (an antonym). This is usually written after the synonyms.

  shy

  Antonym: outgoing

 Find antonyms for these words and write sentences to show their meanings.

expand   generous   mighty   ornate

The Loch Ness Monster

Loch Ness may be the home of an animal as yet unknown to science. Indeed, many scientists still fall over backwards in their efforts to discredit the idea that what is popularly called the Loch Ness Monster could possibly exist. These scientists nervously take refuge behind a barricade of ripples, leaping salmon, shadows, dead stags, logs of wood, branches, and what must surely be the most agile and acrobatic strings of otters ever seen, rather than admit that there is something large, strange and unknown to science in the cold **(1)** of the loch.

Reports of something strange living in Loch Ness are not new. The first mention was by Saint Columba in 565AD, the man who **(2)** Christianity to Scotland. And ever since then there have been stories of the Kelpie or Water Horse, a monster animal that inhabited the loch. There were sightings at the end of the eighteenth century and during the nineteenth, but it was on the afternoon of 14 April 1933, when I was eleven years of age, that the first modern news of the Loch Ness Monster burst upon the world.

To be sure, the local press had reported sightings of an **(3)** animal before this date, but it was the account given by a Mr and Mrs John Mackay of Drumnadrochit that is traditionally credited with being the start of the saga of the monster. They saw – and watched for several minutes – 'an enormous animal rolling and plunging' in the centre of the loch, until it disappeared with a great upsurge of water.

Since then there have been many, many sightings by many, many people. A good number of still photographs have been **(4)**, the most famous perhaps being the 'Surgeon's Photograph', taken in the spring of 1934 by a doctor named Wilson, which clearly shows the animal's raised head and neck emerging from the water.

One thing is certain: there's plenty of room in Loch Ness for large animals. From Fort William at the south end to Inverness at the **(5)**, it runs for twenty-four miles, and it's the third deepest freshwater lake in Europe. In addition, Loch Ness contains ample supplies of food for whatever may live in it. No one can say for sure what is in 'darkest' Loch Ness. You either believe in it or you don't.

Dick King-Smith

A **Write the most suitable word for each number in the passage, from the lines below.**

1. air	waters	banks	waves
2. transported	wished	brought	saw
3. unidentified	electric	outrageous	illegal
4. stolen	lost	misplaced	taken
5. east	top	west	north

 B **Answer these questions.**

1. Give three reasons that scientists put forward to explain the 'monster' sightings.

2. When was a sighting of the Loch Ness Monster first reported?

3. Describe in your own words what the Mackays saw in 1933.

4. Why do you think the number of sightings increased after this?

5. Could the animal be a dinosaur? Give a reason.

6. What is the 'Surgeon's Photograph'?

7. What advantages does Loch Ness offer to a shy monster?

8. Find out about any other mysterious creatures that haven't been properly identified.

 C **True/false assumptions.**

Are these assumptions 'True', 'False' or you 'Don't know'? Discuss your answers.

1. No scientist accepts that the monster exists.

2. Some sightings were dismissed as being shadows.

3. Saint Columba saw the Loch Ness Monster.

4. A horse was seen in the loch.

5. The Mackays made up their story.

D **Do you think the Loch Ness Monster really exists? Write three paragraphs saying why. Refer to the passage and use the following to help you organise your work.**

I think _____   First _____

Next _____   Finally _____

Verbs 1

- A verb is a word that involves doing something or being something.
- Verbs that show action are called action verbs:
  wrote   threw   coughed
- Verbs that do not show action are called linking verbs:
  I **am** tired.
- Remember, verbs must agree with nouns in the singular or the plural:
  David **is** absent, but the other children **are** at school.

 A **Write as many action verbs as you can to describe all your activities at school.**

I am talking, playing ...

 B **Now choose from your words and write three sentences, like this.**

I am talking, but Sean is writing.

 C **We can use many linking verbs to write in the present, past or future tense.**

Write out these sentences so they are complete.
  1. I am shouting and you _____ laughing.
  2. We were jumping but they _____ skipping.
  3. She _____ be going to the party but they _____ be staying at home.
  4. We _____ been to the fair but they _____ been to the cinema.
  5. He _____ bought a new bike, but we still _____ our old ones.

D **Now change these nouns into verbs, as shown.**

argument   argue

hesitation	memory	apology
laughter	complaint	success
confusion	expectation	discussion

Verbs 2

- When we give commands or orders we use verbs in a special way.
  Hurry up!   Be quick!   Come on!

- We stress the verbs and use exclamation marks. What we are really saying is:
  (You) hurry up!   (You) be quick!   (You) come on!

 Think of five expressions we use. Write them down.

- We can also turn sentences into questions by changing the verb, like this:
  I like pancakes.   Do you like pancakes?

B **Read these sentences and turn them into questions.**

1. He has collected the tickets.   **4.** He will make the sandwiches.
2. She has bought the suntan lotion.   **5.** They have packed their bags.
3. I will buy the film.   **6.** It is time to leave.

- When we change tenses we also have to change the linking verb to match.
  He **has** made a cake and he **will** give us a piece of it.

C **Write out these sentences so they are complete.**

1. It _____ sunny today, but yesterday it _____ raining.
2. I _____ looking after the rabbit this week and I _____ look after it
next week.
3. She _____ eaten all the cherries and she _____ eat the banana too.
4. Tomorrow we _____ go to the beach; today we _____staying at home.

- If we change from singular to plural, the verb must also agree.
  She is waiting at the gate. **They were** waiting at the gate.

 Change these sentences from the singular person
to the plural **and the** present **to the** past **tense.**

1. I am taking the dog for a walk.
2. He is painting the hall.
3. She is listening to the programme.

Choosing the Best Adverb

- Usually a thesaurus will not include adverbs ending in **ly**. You will need to form an adverb from the word given.

timid ⟶ timidly

"Where is Rover?" asked Sam.
"I'm afraid he's sitting **timidly** in the corner," replied Jacob.

 A **Continue reading the conversation (dialogue) between Sam and Jacob. The adverbs are missing. Write out the dialogue inserting the most suitable adverb in each space.**

| stubbornly   certainly   anxiously   patiently   quickly |

"Do you think there is something wrong with him?" continued Sam _____.

"Well, he's _____ not as bouncy as usual. I gave him his favourite food and waited _____ but he _____ refused to eat," explained Jacob.

Sam interrupted, "I think we should take him to the vet as _____ as possible."

B **Find a synonym in your thesaurus for each of the words below and turn it into an adverb like this.**

false – **wrong** ⟶ (adverb) – **wrongly**

Remember to write the spelling correctly.

gentle   hungry   happy   silent   excellent   glad   revolting

 C **Continue the story above using the adverbs you have made. Include dialogue.**

There should be three characters. One should be the vet.

Book Reviews

 A **Read this review of *Watership Down* and answer the questions.**

> ### *Watership Down* by Richard Adams
> This is a beautifully written adventure story full of excitement and drama for boys and girls. It traces the adventures of Hazel, the rabbit, and his friends as they travel in search of a new home, encountering many perils and dangers along the way. You'll immediately warm to Hazel and you'll feel you're right there with him on his adventurous journey. It's gripping right to the end. As it's a long and difficult book, I would highly recommend it to readers over the age of 10.

1. What kind of book is *Watership Down*?
2. Did the reviewer enjoy it? Why?
3. Was it recommended for all children?

● The reviewer enjoyed *Watership Down* but sometimes reviewers are critical of books they do **not** like.

 B **Write a critical review of a book which you did not like, using the same format.**

C **Copy the format below and answer the questions to help write your own book review.**

1. **Storyline:** Write a brief synopsis or summary of what happened in the book.
2. **Suitability:** Was the book suitable for your age group? Was it too simple or too hard?
3. **Level of interest:** Was the book interesting and exciting or dull and boring? Which part of the book was the most exciting? Why? What did you not like about the book? Why? What feelings were aroused in you as you read the book?
4. **Characters:** Who was your favourite character? Why did you like him/her/it best? Were the characters well described?
5. **Ending:** Did you like the conclusion? Give reasons for your answer. Did it end tamely or was there a surprise? Do you want to read another book like it?
6. **Recommendation/Rating:** What overall rating out of 10 would you give the book? Do you recommend it for everybody, for particular groups or not at all?

The Lion, the Witch and the Wardrobe

The Lion, the Witch and the Wardrobe *is the story of four children who enter an enchanted land called Narnia through a wardrobe.*

Meanwhile, miles away, the Beavers and the children were walking on into what seemed like a dream. They had left their coats behind them and walked in silence, passing through patches of warm sunlight into cool, green thickets and out again into wide mossy glades where tall elms raised the leafy roof far overhead, and then into dense masses of flowering currant bushes where the sweet smell was almost overpowering.

They had been just as surprised as Edmund when they saw the winter vanishing and the whole world passing in a few hours from winter to spring. They hadn't even known for certain (as the Witch did) that this is what would happen when Aslan came to Narnia.

But they all knew that it was her spells which had produced the endless winter and that when this magic spring began it meant that something had gone badly wrong with the Witch's schemes. After the thaw had been going on for some time they realised that the Witch would no longer be able to use her sledge. After that they didn't hurry so much and they allowed themselves to rest more often.

They had left the course of the big river some time earlier, for one had to turn a little to the south to reach the place of the Stone Table. And now the sun got low and the light got redder and the shadows got longer and the flowers began to think about closing.

Mr Beaver began leading them uphill across some deep springy moss in a place where only tall trees grew, very wide apart.

Just as Lucy was wondering whether she could get to the top without another rest, suddenly they *were* at the top. There was the Stone Table. It was cut all over with strange lines and figures that might be the letters of an unknown language. While they were looking they heard a sound of music on their right, and turning in that direction they saw what they had come to see ...

Aslan stood in the centre of a crowd of creatures. Tree-Women and Well-Women (Dryads and Naiads). There were four great centaurs. There was also a unicorn and a bull with the head of a man and a pelican and an eagle and a great dog. And next to Aslan stood two leopards.

When the children tried to look at Aslan's face, they just caught a glimpse of the golden mane and the great, royal, solemn, overwhelming eyes, and when they found they couldn't look at him they went all trembly.

From *The Lion, the Witch and the Wardrobe*
by C.S. Lewis (abridged by Robin Lawrie)

A **Pick the word from each list that means the same as the bold word.**

1. dense	cool	beautiful	thick	quiet
2. vanishing	strolling	smiling	disappearing	looking
3. schemes	plans	hopes	prayers	feelings
4. solemn	happy	mischievous	angry	serious
5. overpowering	delightful	disgusting	delicious	overwhelming
6. masses	briars	groups	lots	scents

 B **Answer these questions.**

1. Why were the Beavers and the children surprised by what they saw on their journey?
2. Why do you think they left their coats behind?
3. Who was trying to follow the children?
4. Why did they slow down and rest more?
5. List three events which show that nightfall was approaching.
6. Describe what the Stone Table was like and where it was situated.

 C **Heroes and villains.**

1. Write down what you think a hero or heroine is and what a villain is. Check your answers in a dictionary.
2. Think about these questions:
   Who is Aslan?
   What kind of creature is he?
   Is he real or a fantasy?
   Is he a hero or a villain?
3. Write a paragraph describing what he looks like and his personality.
4. What season do you link with Aslan? Why?
5. What other season is described in the passage? Who do you link this season with? Is this creature real or a fantasy? Is it a hero or a villain? Why?

 D **Imagine you have stumbled into an enchanted land.**

Think about who lives there, what the name of the place is, what the weather is like and who the ruler is. Then write what happens.

Indirect Speech

- On page 10 we looked at direct speech, which is the words actually spoken by a person and which are enclosed by speech marks (" ").

  Example: Maeve said, "I will drop by on Monday evening."

- Now we will look at indirect speech, where the words spoken are reported instead of quoted.

  Example: Maeve said that she would drop by on Monday evening.

 Change the statements below from direct speech to indirect speech. (What did Paul whisper? What did Carol say? What did the camper say? What did the cyclist say?)

1. Paul

2. Carol

3. Camper

4. Cyclist

B **Change these sentences to indirect speech.**

1. "May I borrow the pen for a moment?" asked Derek.

2. "The teacher gave us too much homework," complained Ruth and David.

3. "I did not have enough time to do the exercise," protested Sharon.

4. "The patient is to stay in hospital overnight for observation," insisted the doctor.

5. "I hope the goalkeeper will play better in the second half," said Marion.

Adjectives

- On page 18 we learned what nouns are. Adjectives are the colourful words that describe nouns. Now let's see how adjectives tell us more about people, places or things in a sentence.

  Example: The journey was long and painful, but we finally reached the rather isolated, luxurious hotel.

 Write out the two adjectives on each line that best describe the nouns in bold.

film	exciting	delicious	scary	soft
shark	large	timid	dangerous	naughty
doctor	thirsty	wise	thoughtful	spoiled
park	peaceful	handsome	careful	beautiful
room	stubborn	bright	delightful	anxious
thief	valuable	deceitful	luscious	clever

 Make adjectives from the following nouns. Then write a descriptive phrase.

danger *(a dangerous road)*	fury	expense
mystery	anger	misery
poison	skill	storm

C **Use the clues in the context of the passage below to help rewrite the sentences with suitable adjectives in the spaces.**

Mum and Dad had gone out and I was all _____ . Suddenly I heard a crash which seemed to come from the _____ roof. My _____ heart was ready to burst. I raced outside and then I saw a _____ figure, silhouetted against the _____ sky, emerging from the _____ spaceship. Its head was _____ and _____ and it had very _____ arms.
I put on a _____ face and inquired what its name was. "Tiernan" it said; it had come from the _____ planet Jupiter.

Standard English 1

- Remember, when we write in standard English we have to make sure that nouns and verbs agree, like this:

The **parrot has settled** on our roof.

Parrot is the noun, **has settled** is the verb.

 A **Write out these sentences correctly, making sure the verb agrees with the noun.**

1. The eagle soar above the mountains.
2. The thrushes has built a nest on our roof.
3. Our ducks is usually quacking.
4. My friend train his falcon to sit on his arm.
5. His carrier pigeon always return home.

- The subject and the tense of the verb also need to agree.

I climbed up the oak tree to rescue my cat.

I is the subject, **climbed** is the verb in the past tense.

B **Write out and finish these sentences, making sure the subject and the verb agree.**

Use verbs in the past, present and future tenses.

1. The park keeper _____ .
2. Jackie and Pauline _____ on the lake.
3. The football team _____ in the park.
4. Lorraine's dog _____ .
5. We _____ by the park keeper's shed.
6. Along that path, you_____ .
7. I _____ by the park gate.
8. Charlotte and Hayley _____ to a concert.
9. Six groups _____ in the contest.
10. The lion _____ in his cage.
11. Satish _____ in the street.
12. My mum and her friends _____ .

Idioms and Clichés

- An *idiom* is an expression which has a special meaning which cannot be understood by looking at the words separately, e.g. *under the weather* means not well.

- A cliché is an overused expression, often an idiom
  e.g. *sick as a parrot; out like a light.*
  Try not to use them in your writing.

 A **Complete the following idioms. Use the clues in the brackets.**

  1. Over the _____ *(to be overjoyed/happy)*

  2. See the _____ *(become clear/to understand)*

  3. Leave no _____ unturned *(try all possible means)*

  4. Back to _____ one *(go back to the beginning with nothing achieved)*

  5. At a _____ end *(without anything to do)*

B **Read these idioms. What do you think they mean?**

A storm in a teacup
To put the cart before the horse
To cry over spilt milk
A wet blanket
The apple of a person's eye

To put your best foot forward
To hit the nail on the head
To turn over a new leaf
To get into hot water
To beat about the bush
To pour oil on troubled waters
To face the music
To buy a pig in a poke
To let the cat out of the bag
To bury the hatchet
To shed crocodile tears
To blow hot and cold
To put on a brave face
To have your head in the clouds
To wear your heart on your sleeve
To become long in the tooth

Marie Curie

In the autumn of 1891, a 24-year-old Polish student emigrated to Paris and entered the Sorbonne University. She was later to become the woman who has probably made the greatest contribution to science. Her name was Marie Curie. Marie was born in Warsaw in 1867. Both her parents were teachers and at first Marie followed in their footsteps. But she was fascinated by science and became determined to study it properly. She met Pierre Curie, the laboratory chief, at the university. He later became her **(1)**. They lived and worked happily together and became world-famous when they discovered two new elements, polonium and radium, in 1898.

They knew that radium was highly radioactive (giving off invisible rays), and marvelled at its soft glow in the glass containers in which they stored this precious metal. Little did they realise, however, that they, completely unprotected, were handling and working with one of the earth's most dangerous substances. The tragedy was that they were playing with danger and **(2)** their own lives.

Marie and Pierre were awarded the Nobel Prize in 1903. But the danger of working with radium began to take its toll. They both suffered from radiation sickness and their hands were burned whenever they touched **(3)**. In 1906, Pierre was tragically killed when he slipped and fell beneath the wheels of a horse-carriage. Marie was distraught and lonely, but she battled on bravely with her scientific work. She became a professor and was **(4)** a second Nobel Prize in 1911, the first person ever to win two of them for science.

It was during World War One that Marie's work was seen to its greatest effect. She had a radiological car built, which was driven to the battlefront. There she worked with her daughter, Irene, taking X-rays of **(5)** soldiers. They probably saved many lives.

But Marie's own health was fast deteriorating. She was frail and her hands were severely burned. Her other daughter, Eve, nursed her on her death-bed. She died in 1934. The world owes an enormous debt of gratitude to this brilliant woman.

A Write the most suitable word for each
number in the passage, from the lines below.

1. neighbour	husband	enemy	doctor
2. living	enjoying	learning	risking
3. fire	matches	radium	explosives
4. deducted	awarded	provided	inspired
5. wounded	tired	runaway	dead

B Answer these questions.

1. Where is Warsaw? Find it on a map.
2. In what way did Marie follow in her parents' footsteps?
3. Why do you think Marie called one of the elements polonium?
4. Why didn't Marie and Pierre protect themselves from radiation?
5. When did Marie Curie receive her first Nobel Prize?
6. What happened to their hands? What caused this?
7. How did Marie and Irene save soldiers' lives?
8. Find out what importance radium has in today's world.
9. If you could interview Marie, what three questions would you ask her?

C Each numbered sentence tells something that happened
(the effect). In each group, choose the lettered sentence
that tells why or gives a reason (the cause).

1. Marie emigrated to Paris *because*
   a. she hated Poland.
   b. she wanted to study in Paris.
   c. she loved France.
2. Marie Curie died *because*
   a. the radiation sickness killed her.
   b. she didn't eat enough.
   c. of old age.

D When we say something happened in chronological
order we mean it happened in date order.
Draw a timeline of Marie Curie's life.

Put in the important dates and information in order, like this:

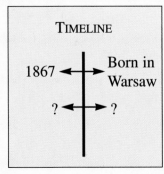

TIMELINE

1867 — Born in Warsaw

? — ?

33

Singular or Plural

- Singular means one person, animal or thing.
- Plural means more than one.

Some rules
1. Many nouns, just add -s, e.g. chairs
2. Nouns ending with ch, sh, s, x, and z add -es, e.g. brushes.
3. Nouns ending with f or fe either add -s, e.g. roofs or change the f(e) to -ves, e.g. halves.

 Rewrite the sentences. Choose suitable nouns from the list in the box and insert them correctly in their plural form.

ceiling	dish	cliff	bell	life	road	thief

1. She began by painting all the _____ first.
2. After dinner, they washed all the dirty _____ .
3. It's very dangerous on the _____ as there's so much traffic on them.
4. The _____ panicked and ran when they heard the alarm _____ ring.
5. The puffins nested close to the bottom of the _____ .
6. Far too many _____ have been lost in war.

Some rules
1. Nouns ending with a consonant followed by y, change the y to ies, e.g. lorries. When y is preceded by a vowel, add -s, e.g. keys.
2. Nouns ending with o, either add -s or -es, e.g. banjos, cargoes.
3. Many plurals must be memorised, e.g. child – children.

 Rewrite these sentences. Insert nouns in their plural form.

echo	volcano	photo	tooth	monkey	city

1. Clouds of smoke belched from the _____ and the ground shook.
2. You could hear the _____ all around the valley when the wolf howled.
3. The _____ jumped from branch to branch and performed tricks.
4. One of the biggest _____ in the world is New York.
5. You should brush your _____ after every meal.
6. I take lots of _____ when I'm on holiday.

Standard English 2

We all speak English in different ways. This partly depends on where we live or who we are talking to. Sometimes different ways of speaking are called dialects. When writers are writing about characters in a story they may want to give them dialects to make them seem real.

For example, a character may say:

"I 'aint done nothing."

In standard English this would be "I haven't done anything."

 Try to work out what the following mean and write them in standard English.

1. "Can we 'ave us books, please?"
2. "They gotten it."
3. "She done it."
4. "Innit?"
5. "Dem mek ya."
6. "Dae ye ken the laddie?"

 Read the following. Write it in standard English.

"Gimme them sweets!" Charlie screamed at the top of his voice.

"They ain't yours!" Andy shouted back.

"Yeah? I seen 'em before you."

"I says they're mine ... I says they're mine ... " chanted Andy, running up the stairs.

Why do you think writers sometimes write in dialect and not in standard English?

 Write some dialect words you know and what they mean in standard English.

 Read the following. Decide which would be in standard English.

1. Writing a letter to a friend.
2. Writing an account of some work you have done to read in assembly.
3. Writing to a shop complaining about something you have bought.
4. Telling a friend about your holiday.

 Choose one that would be written in standard English and write it.

Questions at Night

Why
Is the sky?

What starts the thunder overhead?
Who makes the crashing noise?
Are the angels falling out of bed?
Are they breaking all their toys?

Why does the sun go down so soon?
Why do the night-clouds crawl
Hungrily up to the new-laid moon
And swallow it, shell and all?

If there's a Bear among the stars,
As all the people say,
Won't he jump over those pasture-bars
And drink up all the Milky Way?

Does every star that happens to fall
Turn into a firefly?
Can't it ever get back to heaven at all?
And why
Is the sky?

Louis Untermeyer

 Answer these questions.

1. How would you describe the child's personality?
2. Why does the child think that angels might be 'breaking all their toys'?
3. What does it mean when it says clouds 'swallow' the moon?
4. What do the words 'Bear among the stars' refer to?
5. Why does the poet compare some stars to fireflies?
6. In your own words explain the first and last lines of the poem. What does the child want to know?

 **Thunder is described as 'angels falling out of bed'
and the 'new-laid moon' with its 'shell' is seen as an egg.**

Find interesting ways of describing the following:
a storm cloud   hailstones   a rainbow
Now write your own poem using your own words. You could start: 'Why ... '

Use Your Imagination

 Selling your house.

Find an estate agent's description which is for a house similar to the one you live in. List the adjectives that make the house seem attractive to the buyer.

Now write an estate agent's 'blurb' to sell your own house. Draw a picture of your own house and put your description under it. Decorate it to make it look like an advertisement for selling a house.

 Now write the complete advertisement.

Remember, you probably exaggerated about the house and its facilities.

 Visitors.

Your cousins from overseas are visiting you.

Choose three places in your area that you feel they should visit.

Choose three other places that you would not recommend.

Finally, choose the scariest place in your area for a midnight party.

Now write a diary entry for the day's events. Record the times that they took place and how you all felt.

Example: 11.05am. Cycled to bowling alley. Vicki and I won mega battle.
Munched fries and chicken afterwards. Absolutely brill.

 What do you think the bull is thinking? What do you say to him?

Wuthering Heights

(From the diary of Mr Lockwood)
December 1801.

I have just returned from a visit to my landlord – the only neighbour that I shall be troubled with during my stay at my new home, Thrushcross Grange. This is certainly a beautiful country! In all England, I do not think I could have found a place so wild, so completely apart from the stir of society.

Yesterday afternoon was grey and cold. After a four-mile walk I arrived at my landlord's house, Wuthering Heights, just as the first feathers of snow were falling. Here in North England, 'wuthering' means windy and stormy. The winds must indeed be violent here, as all the trees bend in the same direction, as if begging warmth from the sun. The house is strongly built, with narrow windows. It is very old: over the door I read the date 1500 and the name Hareton Earnshaw.

Shaking with cold, I knocked on the door. Nobody came. At last an old man, clearly a servant, looked out of the window of one of the farm buildings.

"Is there nobody inside to open the door?" I called.

"There's no-one but the missis, and she'll not open it even if you go on knocking till night." He disappeared.

The snow was falling more thickly now. It was bitterly cold. I was about to knock again, when a young man appeared, without a coat, and carrying farm tools. He led me into the living room. It was plainly furnished, but cheerful, with a huge fireplace. On one wall, shelves of great metal dishes and jugs shone in the firelight, and towered row upon row to the roof.

The table was laid for tea, and I was pleased to see 'the missis' sitting there. I bowed and waited for her to speak. She said nothing.

"Rough weather," I smiled.

She never opened her mouth. She just kept her eyes on me in a cool, disagreeable manner.

"Sit down," said the young man, roughly. "Mr Heathcliff will be in soon."

I obeyed, coughed, and repeated my words on the wildness of the weather.

"You should not have come out," said my hostess. She stood up to make tea, and I could now see her clearly. She seemed little more than a child. A perfect figure, and the most beautiful face I have ever seen: very fair, with golden hair. But the expression in her eyes was hard and unhappy.

From *Wuthering Heights* by Emily Brontë (Abridged by Sally Lowe)

Answer these questions.

1. Where is Mr Lockwood's new home? What is it like?
2. What did Mr Lockwood mean by the words 'completely apart from the stir of society'?
3. What time of day did he arrive at Wuthering Heights? Give a reason.
4. Why was the landlord's house named 'Wuthering Heights'?
5. Who first saw Mr Lockwood at Wuthering Heights? What was he like?
6. Describe the living room.
7. What was the young man like?
8. Describe the woman. What did she look like? How did she greet Mr Lockwood?
9. What do you think Mr Heathcliff might be like?

 Write down a word which means the same (a synonym) as each of these.

1. wild
2. violent
3. bitterly
4. disagreeable
5. roughly

 Find words in the passage similar in meaning to the words underlined.

1. The enormous bear <u>rose high up</u> over me.
2. The terrible news <u>disturbed</u> me.
3. All my money <u>vanished</u> into thin air.
4. The crystal chandelier was <u>without fault</u>.

 Tell Mr Lockwood's diary to a friend as if it were the beginning of a story.

Work with a friend.
Read the passage again and refer to your answers in A.
Make notes of the key points in each paragraph.
Check your notes.
Take it in turns to tell each other the passage as though it were the beginning of a long story. Do not look at your notes. You could begin:

'The story I am going to tell you is a strange one ... '

Sentence Contractions

When we read headlines in newspapers or see notices around us they can sometimes have confusing statements. Usually we can guess what they really mean.

 Match the following to their real meanings and write them down by number and letter, like this: 1a or 1b and so on.

Statement	Meaning

1.

Baby Changing Room

a. A place where you can swap your baby for another one.
b. A tiny room for changing your clothes.
c. A place where you can change your baby's nappy.

2.

Police Shoot Man With Knife

a. Police used a knife to shoot a man.
b. Police shot a man who was carrying a knife.

3.

NOTHING ACTS FASTER THAN ANADIN

a. Anadin is an actor who can act quickly.
b. Anadin gives the fastest pain relief.

4.

Go to work on an egg

a. Eat an egg for your breakfast, before going to work.
b. Travel to work sitting on an egg.
c. Eat an egg greedily.

5.

Take the tube

a. Steal a long hollow cylinder.
b. Travel on a long hollow cylinder.
c. Travel on an underground train.

6.

Giant Car Park for Mini Crowd

a. Large car park for people who drive mini cars.
b. Large car park for a small number of people.
c. Car park belonging to a giant for people who drive mini cars.
d. Car park belonging to a giant for a small number of people.

B **Think of your own or find some confusing statements in newspapers, notices or adverts.**

40

What Happened Next?

 Continue this opening paragraph and describe what happened next.

Thor could feel the ground shudder and quake beneath him, as he scurried towards the safety of the cave. Tyrannosaurus bellowed in anger and prowled around the entrance, gnashing his teeth.

   As Thor flopped wearily and crouched in a corner, he wondered how he was going to get home that evening in one piece.

 Diary.

Compile diary entries for an incredible week in your life. Feel free to exaggerate. Follow the example. Write short snappy sentences.

A Week in my Life

Monday Woke at 8 o'clock. Spacecraft landed on roof. Aliens were friendly. Visited their pink planet. Gave me a personal shuttle. Learned how to become invisible. In bed at 10.

 Vary your expression.

The words 'walked' and 'went' are often over-used. Choose five alternatives from the list below and write them in suitable sentences.

marched	scurried	waded
shuffled	hobbled	plodded
scrambled	strolled	galloped
strode	dashed	bounded
wriggled	crawled	hurried

The Space Shuttle

The space shuttle, the first true aerospace vehicle, was developed by NASA, the National Aeronautics and Space Administration, in America. It is the most versatile operated spacecraft ever. For, unlike its predecessors – Mercury, Gemini and Apollo – the shuttle is a reusable spaceship, designed for years of service and capable of making repeated roundtrips to orbit.

The space shuttle system consists of three primary elements: an orbiter spacecraft with three powerful liquid-fuelled main engines, two solid-fuelled booster rockets and an external tank to hold fuel (liquid hydrogen) and oxidizer (liquid oxygen).

Shaped like an aeroplane, the 37.2 metre (122 foot) long orbiter lifts off like a rocket, orbits like a spacecraft and returns to Earth on a landing strip like a glider or an aeroplane. The complex and expensive orbiter is designed to last for at least 100 flights. Five operational orbiters have been built: *Columbia*, *Discovery*, *Atlantis*, *Endeavour* and *Challenger* which along with its crew was sadly lost in an accident on 28 January 1986.

The shuttle provides flexibility never before achieved in space operations, and allows space to be routinely used as the resource it is.

The orbiter's large cargo capacity and relatively mild launch environment enable it to carry into orbit a variety of satellites, including some which could not be launched before because of size, shape, weight or sensitivity to launch forces. Shuttle astronauts have delivered into orbit satellites for communications, Earth observations, scientific research and military purposes. They have recovered and repaired disabled spacecraft and they have dispatched robot probes to the planets. They have conducted medical and other tests to help identify problems and possibilities that might face future space travellers on long-term flights aboard a space station or on a trip to Mars.

When the shuttle era began with the launch of *Columbia* on 12 April 1981, astronauts John Young and Robert Crippen piloted the revolutionary new spaceship on a relatively brief 54-hour test flight that took them 36 times round the world. Commander Young called it a 'dream machine' and the flight duration and size of the crew gradually were increased for later flights.

From Spaceport U.S.A. Tourbook

Find out the meaning of these words. Put them into sentences.

versatile   relatively   observations   revolutionary

 Answer these questions.

1. What main advantage does the shuttle have over its predecessors, Mercury, Gemini and Apollo?
2. What are the three primary elements of the space shuttle?
3. How long is the orbiter spacecraft?
4. Is the space shuttle good value for money? Why?
5. Approximately how long would it take the shuttle to orbit the Earth once?
6. In your own words, explain what shuttle astronauts have succeeded in doing.
7. How do you think an astronaut feels, seconds before blast-off?
8. Design your own spacecraft. Explain why it will be better than the shuttle.
9. Do you think there are inhabitants on Mars? What are your reasons?

C **Read the passage again and the writing frame below.**
Select key information to complete the frame.

Write it out ready to read to a friend or a group.

The Space Shuttle

The space shuttle was developed ...

Unlike those which went before it, the space shuttle is ...

The system consists of ...

The long orbiter ...

Sadly, in ...

It carries satellites for ...

Some other tasks ...

John Young and Robert Crippen ...

43

Where Do the Commas Go?

Read the following. Change the expression of your voice when you read the part of the sentence which is written in bold.

Everything, **including the spectacular pink birthday cake**, was ready for the party.

Sometimes when we are writing more complicated sentences we use commas around additional information.

 Decide where the commas go in these sentences and write them out.

Read each sentence with expression.

1. Joe who was never on time rushed around the kitchen.
2. Lizzie and Janie known as the terrible tigers were arguing with each other.
3. Grandma lying fast asleep in the chair had dropped her spectacles.
4. The baby who was always happy gurgled and cooed like a little bird.
5. Lennie as well as making the tea and toast had boiled the eggs.
6. Mum while watching the scene in front of her laughed at the family.

 Write down and complete the following sentences about the family. Use two commas in each sentence.

1. The dog ...
2. The guinea pig ...
3. Reggie ...
4. The letters ...
5. Nobody ...
6. All the family ...

44

Adverbs

- Adverbs usually describe and tell us more about verbs. Adverbs are often formed by adding -ly or -ily to an adjective. These tell how an action was done. *Example:* wrote neatly; sang beautifully.

A Rewrite the sentences. Make adverbs from the adjectives on the left.

1. slow   The boat drifted *slowly* downstream.
2. noisy   The monkeys chattered _____ .
3. reckless The drunken motorist drove _____ .
4. greedy   The escaped convict _____ devoured the meat.
5. grateful I _____ accepted the gift.
6. awkward   Huck Finn shuffled _____ out of the room.
7. diligent The farmer struggled _____ to make ends meet.
8. humble   The telephone caller _____ apologised.

- Adverbs may also tell where or when an action took place. *Example:* She seldom drives.

B Rewrite the passage. Choose suitable adverbs from the box below.

| immediately | repeatedly | early |
| everywhere | outside | rarely |

It was dark when James woke _____ one morning and went _____ into the garden. He was _____ hearing a noise from the shed. He jumped over the wall and _____ headed towards the noise.

He waited near the door and listened to the racket that was coming from within. As he pushed the door open, something brushed past him and ran into the darkness. He walked into the shed and _____ had he seen such a sight. There were feathers _____ . The fox had paid his yearly visit.

C Write adverbs that are *opposite* in meaning to those used below.

1. The sun shone **brightly**.
2. The ball **narrowly** missed the window.
3. Our aunt **seldom** forgets our birthdays.
4. The teacher looked at me **sympathetically**.
5. The mechanic **carefully** replaced the engine.

Action Paragraphs

- Once you've decided on how you're going to open a story, the next step is to describe the main action that took place. It's important to use exciting verbs (action words) and adverbs, so that the reader can visualise what you're describing.

- **Problem/goal**

  The characters in your story will possibly face some danger or problem, such as being lost in the woods. Or they may be trying to achieve some goal, such as trying to discover gold. Choose one main idea for your story and indent the first line of each paragraph.

 Look at the pictures below. Then write three paragraphs which describe what happened in each picture.

 Copy the words below, filling in the missing noun, verb or adverb on the left. Then write interesting action sentences, using all the words.

1. snake	hissed	fiercely:	The snake hissed fiercely at our dog.
2.	crept	stealthily:	
3. teacher	smiled		
4.	swam	gracefully:	
5. sister	shrieked		
6.	stumbled	awkwardly:	
7.	sulked		
8.		impatiently:	
9. bull			
10.	examined		
11. bird	sang		
12.	howled		

Spelling Rules

The rules on this page will help you remember spellings.

- When the word **full** is added to another word we drop one **l** like this:
  full   care**ful**

 Write out the answers to these word sums.

use + full =   grate + full =
hate + full =   pain + full =
hope + full =   power + full =
thank + full =   faith + full =
wonder + full =   spoon + full =

Choose words to write six sentences. You can use more than one word in a sentence if you want.

B Can you guess what happens to full and fill and also un and till when they are added together? Write down your answers.

- When a word has a short vowel you double the consonant before adding **ing**, like this: **tap + ing = tapping**.

C Write out the answers to these word sums.

run + ing =
hop + ing =
pin + ing =
hum + ing =
pat + ing =
swim + ing =
skip + ing =

D Think of four more words with short vowel sounds and add ing to them.

- Remember words with long vowels such as hope and pine do not double the consonant.
  hope + **ing** = **hoping**

The Sheep-Pig

The Sheep-Pig *is the remarkable story of a pig named Babe, which was 'adopted' by Farmer Hogget's old sheepdog, Fly. Friendly and popular with the sheep, Babe gradually became an expert at rounding them up for the farmer.*

What a sight greeted him when he arrived in the far field! The flock, usually so tightly bunched, was scattered everywhere, eyes bulging, mouths open, heads hanging in their evident distress, and it was clear that the dogs had been at their worrying for some time. A few sheep had tried in their terror to jump the wire fencing and had become caught up in it, some had fallen into the ditches and got stuck. Some were limping as they ran about, and on the grass were lumps of wool torn from others.

Most dreadful of all, in the middle of the field, the worriers had brought down a ewe, which lay on its side feebly kicking at them as they growled and tugged at it.

On the day when the rustlers had come, Babe had felt a mixture of fear and anger. Now he knew nothing but a blind rage, and he charged flat out at the two dogs, grunting and snorting with fury. Nearest to him was the smaller dog, a kind of mongrel terrier, which was snapping at one of the ewe's hindlegs, deaf to everything in the excitement of the worry.

Before it could move, Babe took it across the back and flung it to one side, and the force of his rush carried him on into the bigger dog and knocked it flying.

This one, a large black crossbred, part collie, part retriever, was made of sterner stuff than the terrier, which was already running dazedly away; and it picked itself up and came snarling back at the pig. Perhaps, in the confusion of the moment, it thought that this was just another sheep that had somehow found courage to attack it; but if so, it soon knew better, for as it came on, Babe chopped at it with his terrible pig's bite, the bite that grips and tears, and now it was not sheep's blood that was spilled.

Howling in pain, the black dog turned and ran, his tail between his legs. He ran, in fact, for his life, an open-mouthed bristling pig hard on his heels.

The field was clear, and Babe suddenly came back to his senses. He turned and hurried to the fallen ewe, round whom, now that the dogs had gone, the horrified flock was beginning to gather in a rough circle. ... It was Ma! "Ma!" he cried. "Ma! Are you all right?" She did not seem too badly hurt. ... The old ewe opened an eye. Her voice, when she spoke, was as hoarse as ever, but now not much more than a whisper.

"Hullo, young 'un," she said.

From *The Sheep-Pig* by Dick King-Smith

Answer these questions.

1. The dogs were 'at their worrying'. Explain what this means.

2. Describe in your own words how the sheep reacted.

3. What is a ewe?

4. Why do you think the ewe kicked only 'feebly' at the dogs?

5. Use three different words to describe how Babe felt.

6. Why did he feel that way?

7. What does the phrase 'made of sterner stuff' mean?

8. How might the dogs have felt when they thought about the pig attacking them?

9. Do you think that the old ewe will live? Give a reason.

10. Have you ever done anything in a 'blind rage'? Describe it.

B **The passage tells us what was happening from Babe's point of view.**

Write two paragraphs saying what happened from these characters' points of view:

the terrier dog   Ma, the old ewe

Imagine you are the animal. Use the pronoun 'I'.

C **Word meanings.**

Find these words from the passage in your dictionary and put them in suitable sentences:

terror   distress   evident   horrified   dreadful   bristling

 Try to see the film _Babe_.

1. When we are talking about film we sometimes use the word 'animation'. What does it mean?

2. Think of an example of animation in _Babe_.

3. Do you think that using animation was a good idea or not? Explain your answer.

4. Think of two characters that seemed the same to you in both the book and the film. Say why.

5. Think of one character that seemed different in the film and say why.

Homophones

● 'Homophones' are words that sound alike but are different in spelling and meaning, e.g. **Flower** = part of a plant; **Flour** = substance used in cooking.

A Give a homophone for each of the following.

bare	hole	maid
seller	right	bough
wood	ewe	night
hare	quay	hymn
none	prophet	pair
wait	blew	waist

B Choose the correct word from the list. Complete the sentences.

ate	profit	hole	new
our	ewe	wood	whole
knew	eight	through	prophet
would	hour	yew	threw

1. It was _____ o'clock before I _____ some food.
2. Everyone _____ that he had bought a _____ car.
3. She _____ the ball _____ the window.
4. _____ flight was delayed by one _____ .
5. The miser buried the _____ lot of his savings in a deep _____ at the end of the field.
6. A _____ isn't a business person so he/she doesn't get a _____ .
7. The ram and the _____ stood near the _____ tree.
8. We _____ like to go for a stroll in the _____ later.

C Write the correct words.

part of a face – is familiar with: nose/knows

male child – shines in the sky s_____/s_____   of glass – ache p_____/p_____

for a dock – for a lock q_____/k_____   not me! – female sheep y_____/e_____

quietness – a part of p_____/p_____   of a ship – to sell s_____/s_____

seven days – feeble w_____/w_____   to pull – part of the foot t_____/t_____

sixty minutes – belongs to us h_____/o_____   expensive – an animal d_____/d_____

50

Soft c

- Sometimes **c** can sound hard like **k**: cot cage company
- Sometimes it can sound soft like **s**: space city cycle
- Remember **c** is usually soft in a word when it is followed by **e**, **i** or **y**.

 A **Write out the soft c words in this paragraph.**
Put them under three lists: ce, ci and cy.

It was summer and Sameera was riding her bicycle along the city streets at a fast
pace towards the circus, which had recently returned from France. She cycled
near the swans and cygnets on the lake and circled the roundabout. For once
there was plenty of space and she whistled to herself, excited at the chance of
getting a ticket at the right price to see the world-famous acrobat, Cecile. As she
raced towards the entrance she saw a notice pinned to a fence in the distance.
She could see something was wrong and on coming closer she read, 'Show
cancelled due to unforeseen circumstances. Apologies from the Management.'
Sameera sighed, turned and giving the
words a backward glance,
decided it would have to be
the cinema again.

Letter Strings

 A **ough has different sounds. Read the sayings and say the sound in the ough words.**

1. a rough ride   **2.** a thorough clean   **3.** a cough and a cold
4. through the tunnel   **5.** second thoughts   **6.** ploughing the fields
7. although there were two ...

B **Match the sayings in A which have the same ough sound with those in B. (Match them by number and letter.)**

a) the borough team   **b)** he fought like a dog   **c)** three jam doughnuts
d) the pig's trough   **e)** a tough cookie   **f)** a summer drought
g) through space

C **Write your own sayings, using these words: brought, ought, bought.**

D **oo can also have different sounds. Say these words: moon, boot, pool.**

Most people say these words differently: book, door.
Try to hear the difference and pair them with these words: poor, hook.
Write down the pairs.

E **Now write down the oo word that sounds different in each of these lists.**

1. too   room   noon   look   cool

2. soon   boom   root   loop   wood

3. food   roof   cook   hoot   doom

4. loose   soot   fool   school   goose

Write sentences, using the words you have written down. Read them to a friend.

Possessive Pronouns

- We use these words to show that something belongs to someone:

my   mine   your   yours   his   her   hers   its   our   ours   their   theirs

 Choose the correct word for each sentence and write it down.

Read the sentences through again.

1. Amy returned home and hung up *(her/his)* red jacket.

2. Ned, Amy's brother, hung *(his/hers)* red jacket in the hall next to *(his/hers)*.

3. Later, Amy picked up what she thought was *(her/his)* red jacket and went into town.

4. Ned left to meet Amy and put on Amy's red jacket, which he thought was *(his/hers)*.

5. When the two met outside the cinema, they stared at *(their/our)* red coats.

6. "Is that red jacket *(my/mine)*?" exclaimed Amy.

7. "Don't you mean, is this red jacket *(ours/yours)*?" laughed Ned.

8. "Well I'll swap *(my/mine)* for *(your/yours)*!" they both said together.

 Make up a short dialogue about missing a train.

Use possessive pronouns, including these:

its   our   ours   theirs

Natural Disasters

The earth is a restless and sometimes violent world to live in. Every year brings its share of natural **(1)**. Avalanches of snow are common and deadly mountain hazards. They can occur even on slight slopes. Avalanches can be triggered off by earth tremors, loud noises, or even people walking on loose snow. They can also start spontaneously, especially in spring as the deep winter snowfalls begin to melt. Avalanches are fearful sights; thundering along at speeds of over 320km/h they can flatten forests and **(2)** whole villages.

Deadly avalanches killed over 8500 soldiers in Italy in 1916. The havoc caused by avalanches is a dreadful reminder of the immense forces of nature.

Earthquakes usually occur where the plates of the earth's crust grind against each other. This causes tension in the rocks and when it becomes too great they shift and split. The rock movements cause shock waves which start deep underground. The point on the surface above is called the epicentre and is the scene of **(3)** destruction, but shock waves travel out from the epicentre just as ripples spread out when you drop a stone into a pond.

Earthquakes in China have caused terrible loss of life; the worst, in 1556, killed over 800 000 people.

Scientists are trying to find ways of **(4)** earthquakes so that people can be warned to leave danger areas in time. Animals may offer a clue; it is claimed that they behave oddly before quakes, perhaps sensing changes unnoticed by people.

Wind is just moving air, but when it races along at 500km/h, as in a tornado, its destructive violence is terrifying. Tornadoes are also called twisters, because the air twists, or spins. A snaking funnel of cool air sinks down from a cloud. Warm air whirls up the funnel at fantastic speed, sucking up anything in its path, from houses to railroad cars. Objects caught in a tornado's path are totally **(5)**, exploding in the partial vacuum at the centre of the twister, though buildings just to the side of the tornado's narrow passage are untouched. Fortunately tornadoes are rare except in the Midwest of America.

Hurricanes are tropical storms 'fuelled' by warm, moist air above the sea. They whirl more slowly than tornadoes but cover a larger area. The high winds are dangerous enough but the greatest threat of hurricanes is that they carry torrential rain and drive massive waves before them.

From *Exploring the Violent Earth* by Jonathan Rutland

54

A **Write the most suitable word for each number in the passage, from the lines below.**

1. colours	flavours	headaches	disasters
2. improve	bury	visit	paint
3. least	nicest	greatest	smallest
4. stopping	beating	forecasting	slowing
5. welcomed	rebuilt	secure	destroyed

 B **Answer these questions.**

1. Why are avalanches mainly mountain hazards?
2. Why do some avalanches start in spring?
3. Explain in your own words how earthquakes occur.
4. What damage have you seen that was caused by earthquakes?
5. What do you think some animals do when they sense an earthquake is about to occur?
6. What film begins with a tornado sweeping a house 'somewhere over the rainbow'?
7. Why do you think objects and buildings explode in the central vacuum?
8. What is the difference between a hurricane and a tornado?
9. Which of the three natural disasters would you least like to be involved in? Why?

● When we are given information the writer sometimes uses technical vocabulary.

 C **Explain the technical vocabulary below.**

tremor   shock waves   vacuum

Check in a dictionary.

 D **Find out about typhoons, from library books or ICT.**

Use contents pages and indexes or a CD-ROM to find information.

Select four points.

In your own words write a paragraph about each point.

Asking Questions

- Remember you must use a question mark at the end of a sentence which asks a question.

 Write suitable questions for these answers and don't forget to use capital letters where necessary.

1. It's just after three o'clock.
2. No, Gary was not at school today.
3. I don't know who did it.
4. She left it on the table.
5. He was living in Paris then.
6. I haven't seen them since Christmas.
7. It's about ten miles from here.
8. It stopped because we ran out of fuel.
9. I am a hundred and one years old.

Compound Words

- Two separate words can be joined in order to make a compound word, e.g. grand + mother = grandmother.

 The letters of each individual word have been scrambled. Arrange them in the correct order so as to write a compound word.

eta + nsopo = ?   pamc + ites = ?

refi + rmas = ?   deirb + mogor = ?

mtei + nlei = ?   erkab + gtohuhr = ?

rbfei + seca = ?   daroi + cevati = ?

ktcar + utsi = ?   trbtue + lifse = ?

srocs + wbo = ?   kcalb + drabo = ?

Suffixes – sion, tion and cian

● The suffixes **sion**, **tion** and **cian** all sound **shun**.

 A **Sort the following under the three spelling patterns.**

magician	explosion	consideration	decision
revision	occasion	illusion	electrician
invasion	detention	collection	imagination
invitation	seclusion	intrusion	composition
superstition	musician	relation	provision

 B **Choose from the words, match them to these meanings and write them down.**

1. sudden violent noise, bursting outwards
2. a piece of writing or music which has been composed
3. a group of items
4. to be kept in a place without being free to go
5. special event

 C **Finish and write down the sentences, using the two words given.**

1. All at once the ... *(magician, illusion)*
2. I had to ... *(decision, electrician)*
3. Yesterday ... *(invitation, relation)*
4. He knew ... *(superstition, imagination)*

Finish the Story

- You need to think about how you are going to finish a story. First read this passage carefully.

Commander Ericson and her crew were eagerly looking forward to meeting their families again. Their experience on the space station, Plato, isolated from all communications with Earth, had proven a resounding success. They had survived despite many difficulties. But the experiment's findings would have to wait for later analysis. The starship stormed into the Earth's atmosphere and Commander Ericson immediately turned on the video scanner for the first time in five years. The crew gathered around, straining to catch a glimpse of their home planet. However, they were horrified and awestruck by the scenes that greeted them.

 Think about these questions.

When is the story set, present or future?
What do you think has horrified and shocked the crew? How did it happen?
What choices now face Commander Ericson and her crew?
Will the crew survive? Why do you think so?
Could there be a simple explanation for the scenes which greeted them?

 By thinking about questions such as these, you'll be in a position to finish a story properly. Now write your ending to the above story.

Meeting a New Face

- A new family has just moved into the house next door to you. As you peep from behind the curtains, you notice that one member of the family is about your age. You decide to introduce yourself when you see him/her in the back garden. How might you first attract his/her attention?

 Write the conversation you had with your new neighbour.

Words Often Confused

- 'Passed' is a verb, e.g. The goalkeeper passed the ball to me.
- 'Past' is usually used **with** a verb, e.g. The rally car flashed past our house.
- The easiest test is that you can only put **I, you**, **he**, **she**, **it**, **we**, **you** and **they** in front of the verb (passed) for it to make sense.

A **Rewrite the passage. Fill in the spaces with either 'passed' or 'past'.**

The escaped prisoner, Annie – The Wild One, drove _____ the startled guards at high speed. She entered the highway and almost immediately _____ a police car. When the driver saw her roaring _____ , he almost collapsed.

Shortly afterwards, Annie sped _____ the bank that she'd robbed and dropped a message out of the window. It read, 'Annie _____ through town. You don't have to worry. My robbing days are all in the _____ '. The bank manager almost _____ out when she read it.

Meanwhile, the prison authorities _____ on the message to the mayor. He looked out of the window just in time to see Annie zoom _____ his office. Crowds cheered as the daredevil fugitive _____ a final roadblock and disappeared in a cloud of smoke.

B **Write a homophone (a word that sounds the same) for every word below.**

tern	steel	principal	no	hair
check	waist	wood	rain	beach	practice

C **Write down the word in each line that is similar in meaning to the word in bold.**

1. innocent:	perfect	simple	blameless	good
2. harmony:	jealousy	agreement	laughter	permission
3. luscious:	deep	delicious	ambitious	rich
4. jagged:	notched	sharp	diagonal	irregular

D **Write down the word that does not belong on each line.**

1. doctor	surgeon	nurse	taxidermist	dentist
2. remember	recognise	identify	acknowledge	rupture
3. furious	angry	devastated	raging	violent

Little House on the Prairie

As they made their way to the prairie, where they built their little house, the Ingalls family encountered many obstacles and dangers along the way.

Pet and Patty lifted their wet noses. They pricked their ears forward, looking at the creek; then they pricked them backward to hear what Pa would say. They sighed and laid their soft noses together to whisper to each other.

The wagon went forward softly in mud. Water began to splash against the wheels. The splashing grew louder. The wagon shook as the noisy water struck at it. Then all at once the wagon lifted and balanced and swayed. It was a lovely feeling. The noise stopped, and Ma said, sharply, "Lie down, girls!" Quick as a flash, Mary and Laura dropped flat on the bed. When Ma spoke like that, they did what they were told. Ma's arm pulled a smothering blanket over them, heads and all.

Mary did not move; she was trembling and still. But Laura could not help wriggling a little bit. She did so want to see what was happening. She could feel the wagon swaying and turning; the splashing was noisy again, and again it died away. Then Pa's voice frightened Laura. It said, "Take them, Caroline!" The wagon lurched; there was a sudden heavy splash beside it. Laura sat straight up and clawed the blanket from her head.

Pa was gone. Ma sat alone, holding tight to the reins with both hands. Mary hid her face in the blanket again, but Laura rose up farther. She couldn't see the creek bank. She couldn't see anything in front of the wagon but water rushing at it. And in the water, three heads; Pet's head and Patty's head and Pa's small wet head. Pa's fist in the water was holding tight to Pet's bridle.

Laura could faintly hear Pa's voice through the rushing of the water. It sounded calm and cheerful, but she couldn't hear what he said. He was talking to the horses. Ma's face was white and scared.

For a long, long time the wagon swayed and swung, and Mary cried without making a sound, and Laura's stomach felt sicker and sicker. Then the front wheels stuck and grated, and Pa shouted. The whole wagon jerked and jolted and tipped backward, but the wheels were turning on the ground. Laura was up again, holding on to the seat; she saw Pet's and Patty's scrambling wet backs climbing a steep bank and Pa running beside them, shouting, "Hi, Patty! Hi, Pet! Get up! Get up! Whoopsy-daisy! Good girls!"

At the top of the bank they stood still, panting and dripping. And the wagon stood still, safely out of that creek.

Laura Ingalls Wilder

Answer these questions.

1. What obstacle did the Ingalls family encounter in this passage?
2. Why did the wagon lift, balance and sway?
3. Why did the children obey their mother's instruction immediately?
4. What caused Laura to become so frightened? What did she do then?
5. What was Ma's first name?
6. What could Laura see in front of the wagon?
7. Why do you think Pa spoke so calmly and cheerfully to the horses?
8. What differences do you notice between Laura's and Mary's personalities?
9. Did Ma and Pa succeed? How? What might have gone wrong?
10. Did Laura and Mary help their parents in any way? What would you have done?

 Word meanings.

Write in your own words what the following words from the passage mean.
swayed   smothering   lurched   bridle   panting

 There are many verbs in the passage ending in ing.
They help to create a feeling of action.

Find and write down ten verbs ending in **ing**.
Say them quickly one after the other. Write down what they sound like.

 Some words in the passage that are close together
begin with the same sound, like 'swayed and swung'.
We call this alliteration (al-lit-er-a-tion).

1. Find words that are close together beginning with 'j' and write them down.
2. Think of your own alliteration using 'j'. Use your words in sentences.

 Use your imagination.

Describe how you rescued somebody or an animal from drowning.

Antonyms

Some words are opposite in meaning to others. These are called **antonyms**.

Example: aunt / uncle

 A **Pair the antonyms from these lists and write them out.**

warm   child   sister   better   me   west   asleep   him   buy   singular

plural   sell   cool   her   brother   adult   east   awake   worse   you

 B **Find pairs of words that have the same meaning (synonyms) from the lists below and write them down.**

less   grubby   rich   recall   tiny   old   expensive   away

ancient   wealthy   dear   dirty   fewer   remember   small   far

Now read these antonyms:

more   large   cheap   poor   modern   near   clean   forget

Match each pair of synonyms to their antonym, like this:

less, fewer – more

 C **Make opposites by adding the correct prefixes un, dis, mis to these words.**

advantage   behave   kind   content   wise   aware   connect   direct

● We can also make opposites in our writing by using groups of words.

I was **late** for the appointment.   I was **on time** for the appointment.

 D **Write pairs of sentences using the following.**

come/go back   parted/brought together   concealed/opened up

Descriptions

 A **Vary your expression.**

- The word 'nice' is overworked when describing people.
- Use the more descriptive words from the box to describe the people below.

thoughtful	generous	hospitable	angelic	gentle
amusing	sympathetic	considerate	polite	friendly

 B **The sky-jump. Write short answers to these questions.**

You're about to sky-jump from an aeroplane.

- How do you feel? What do you see? What do you hear?
- You jump out and start to free-fall. What sensation do you experience?
- When you pull the cord, the parachute does not open at first. How do you react?
- Eventually it opens and you float down towards a beach. What does it look like from above?
- You land safely and some children come running towards you. What do they say to you?
- Will you do it again? Why?

 C **This bull's name is Bellowface.**
Think of appropriate names to call:

his mother	his brother	his sister
his father	his wife	his friend

Think of three different reasons why Bellowface is angry. Then write them down.

Onomatopoeia

When a word sounds like its meaning we call this **onomatopoeia**.
(on – o – mat – o – poei – a).

 Write down what these words remind you of.

bang!	clash!	splat!	smack!	trickle!	swoop!
snip-snap!	scamper	flip	crunch	rumble	flit

 Make up names to match these characters.

The first has been done for you.

 Read this poem.

Splish Splosh!

Drip drop
Tinkle
Slip slop
Sprinkle
Splish splosh
Slap slosh
Splash bash crash!
Mary Green

Mr Chuckle

 **Now make up a poem,
choosing from the following:**

a car with a puncture
a bike with a loose chain
a horse without a shoe
a steam train building up speed
playing table-tennis and losing the ball

Figures of Speech

- When we are talking to people we often use expressions or figures of speech. These are groups of words that are put in place of other words.

- When we say: It's raining cats and dogs, we mean it's raining very heavily. We don't mean that cats and dogs are falling from the sky!

 Match the following everyday comments to their meanings by writing down the correct number and letter.

1. We're in the same boat.	**a.** a miserable or discouraging person
2. Tell me, I'm all ears.	**b.** to be rude
3. You'll get into hot water.	**c.** to stop something quickly
4. I smell a rat.	**d.** to be similar to a parent
5. She's always putting her foot in it.	**e.** to start again and behave better
6. I've promised to turn over a new leaf.	**f.** to be listening carefully
7. You need to knock that on the head.	**g.** to get into trouble
8. Don't be such a wet blanket.	**h.** to be suspicious
9. He's a chip off the old block.	**i.** to be in the same situation
10. Don't give me any backchat.	**j.** to upset somebody, without thinking

 Read the following and write a dialogue between Deepak and Bilu. Use one or two figures of speech to show this is an ordinary conversation.

There has been a long-running argument between Deepak and his friend Bilu. Usually they share everything, but Deepak is reluctant to lend his new bike to Bilu, whose own bike has a puncture.

Deepak:

Bilu:

Changing Sentences

● We can write the same sentence in different ways and combine two or more sentences into one. Sometimes words are lost or changed, as in the examples below:

Philip closed the window. **He drew** the curtains.
Philip closed the window **and** drew the curtains.
Philip closed the window **before drawing** the curtains.
Philip drew the curtains **after closing** the window.

 Combine these sentences in two different ways.

1. Fiona put down the cutlery. She turned off the television.
2. Darren brought in the plate of sandwiches. He placed them on the table.
3. Lena washed the cups. She made the tea.

 Now rewrite these paragraphs, saying the same thing in a different way.

You can add, remove and change words, but you must keep to the meaning of the passage. Do not write too many short sentences.

1. The children's mother came into the hall and took off her coat. She stroked the cat and went into the living room. She saw what the children had done and smiled broadly. The supper was ready and she could rest her weary feet.

2. The rain had not stopped falling all day. Paul did not mind because he wanted to read anyway. At least the rain gave him a good excuse. Unfortunately the door bell rang and it was Leroy, Paul's best friend. Paul looked longingly at his book as they went upstairs to play on his computer.

3. The princess, thought her chief servant, does not know how to do anything but moan. She was never satisfied. Heaven knows they had been as attentive as possible when the prince refused to marry her. She seemed determined to take the rejection out on them, however. There was her bell again and he began to wonder whether to type or write his resignation letter.

In Agreement

 A **Make four columns: common noun, pronoun, proper noun and collective noun.**

Read the passage and write examples of the different nouns in the correct column.

Josie's team ran on to the pitch and took their places. They were keen to begin the game while it was still sunny. Billy's band of contestants followed and there was much cheering from the smaller pupils. The group of children who were not playing stood at one corner of the field chatting. Finally, Mr Godber blew the whistle ...

 B **Read this passage. Write down why you think it sounds strange.**

Leon plunged into the water from the top diving board and swam steadily towards the opposite end of the swimming pool. Leon hoped to be able to manage thirty lengths if he could. Yesterday, Leon had swum twenty-eight, even though Leon had been tired.

Write out the passage, changing certain words to make it sound better. What is the grammatical name of the words you have chosen?

 C **Read the following sports commentary.**

Davis is in the lead, having passed Grimshaw. Each is rounding the bend into the final lap. A supporter is waving his hat as Grimshaw speeds forward, but Davis keeps going. It's going to be closer than I thought ... !

Write out the passage turning the singular into the plural. Make sure the verbs and pronouns agree. You can add words like this:

Davis and Goldstein are in the lead ...

Interesting Sentences

 Combine the three words on each line to form an interesting sentence.

Example: injured – driver – groaned

The injured driver groaned as he was lifted onto the stretcher.

1. refugees – trudged – wearily   **2.** majestic – eagle – soared

3. curious – tourists – explored   **4.** eyes – glinted – merrily

5. boy – muttered – sulkily   **6.** hostile – natives – threatened

7. colossal – dinosaur – pounded   **8.** patient – struggled – painfully

9. customer – grumbled – angrily   **10.** startled – rabbit – scurried

 Write some sentences.

You were looking around inside an old deserted house. You touched a part of the fireplace and a trapdoor opened up. You could see stone steps leading down into a dark passageway. How did you feel? What did you do? What did you see?

 Now copy the table below. Try filling in the missing adjective, verb or adverb of your choice. Then write an interesting sentence using all the words on each line.

Example: hungry dog devoured greedily

The hungry dog greedily devoured its dinner.

Adjective	Noun	Verb	Adverb
1.	train	rumbled	
2.	door		noisily
3. drunken	man		
4.	waves		violently
5.	salmon	leaped	
6. fierce	lion		
7.	thief	crept	
8.	child		politely
9. energetic	athlete		
10.	teacher		suspiciously

Country Cat

'Where are you going, Mrs Cat,
All by your lonesome lone?'
'Hunting a mouse, or maybe a rat
Where the ditches are overgrown.'

'But you're very far from your house and home,
You've come a long, long way –'
'The further I wander, the longer I roam
The more I find mice at play.'

'But you're very near to the dark pinewood
And foxes go hunting too.'
'I know that a fox might find me good,
But what is a cat to do?

I have my kittens who must be fed,
I can't have them skin and bone!'
And Mrs Cat shook her brindled head
And went off by her lonesome lone.

Elizabeth Coatsworth

 Answer these questions.

1. Why was Mrs Cat hunting?
2. What does the expression 'skin and bone' mean?
3. Why is it dangerous for her to hunt 'near to the dark pinewood'?
4. Find out the word that describes animals that hunt mainly at night.
5. Write three sentences describing Mrs Cat's personality.

 Read the poem again.

1. Find two groups of words that are repeated.
2. Write down words that rhyme with 'Cat', 'home', 'play', 'good', 'too', 'head'.
   Say where they come in the line.
3. Choose the best word you think describes this poem when you read it:
   slow, rolling, flat, quick, clever, steady.

 Write a poem which begins:

'Where are you going, Mr Fox?'

Bigfoot

The Hendersons were driving home from a disastrous camping trip when a huge creature emerged from nowhere to make a big impression on them.

Nancy looked around for a place for Bigfoot to sit while she worked on his injured hand. The chairs were too fragile, and she didn't want to risk the counters. Finally, she settled him on the kitchen floor, with his back against the refrigerator for support. Nancy was glad to see his cuts weren't too deep. He was patient while she washed them out with soap and water.

Ernie returned with the first-aid kit. After a week's camping, it was hopelessly disorganised. The only antiseptic Nancy could find was iodine.

Nancy spoke soft and low to Bigfoot, a kind of singing. She recognised the voice as one she hadn't used much since her kids got older. "Now this might hurt, just a little."

The creature was nearly hypnotised into trust. Nancy soaked a gauze pad with iodine and took the creature's hand. He looked at her sheepishly, then squeezed his eyes shut tight. "It's okay, it's okay," Nancy crooned. Still she felt the creature's hand wince when the iodine stung the cuts.

"Does this mean we can keep him?" Ernie asked in a voice that was unusually quiet for Ernie.

"Grow up!" Sarah said.

George said, "Maybe ... I don't know." He said it with a hint of a question mark at the end.

Nancy looked up from her doctoring. "You don't know? The answer's no. Now you know."

"It was just so different when he was dead," George mused.

Nancy looked sharply at him. "No, George. *You* were different. And I was convinced it wasn't dead."

Sarah spoke up. "I thought we were going to sell it and get rich."

"Let's *keep* it and get rich," Ernie suggested.

"I can't believe this family," Nancy said. What she couldn't believe was their insensitivity. Oh sure, she was always the bleeding heart, always the soft one, but somebody had to be. Enough was enough. Bigfoot growled, and Nancy realised she'd been playing too roughly with the iodine. "I'm sorry," she told him.

Joyce Thompson

Answer these questions.

1. Why had Nancy difficulty in finding a place for Bigfoot to sit?
2. What injuries did Bigfoot have?
3. Do you think the Hendersons used the first-aid kit regularly? How do you know?
4. What tone of voice did Nancy use when speaking to the creature?
5. Was Bigfoot intelligent? Did he like the Hendersons? How do you know?
6. What do we learn about Sarah's attitude towards Bigfoot? Had Ernie similar feelings?
7. When do you think George felt that Bigfoot was dead?
8. How did Nancy feel about the way in which her family discussed Bigfoot's future?
9. What plan would you have proposed, if you were a Henderson?

 In each group, choose the letter which finishes the sentence correctly.

1. The injuries Bigfoot received: **a.** crippled him for life.
  b. caused him to shut his eyes permanently.
  c. made him wince.

2. Bigfoot was hypnotised into trust because:
  a. the iodine put him to sleep.
  b. the pain knocked him out.
  c. Nancy's voice soothed and reassured him.

3. The Hendersons decided: **a.** to sell Bigfoot and get rich.
  b. to keep him for a while.
  c. to hand him over to the police.

 Use your dictionary, if necessary, to match the words on the left with their correct meanings. Then write them in suitable sentences.

1. antiseptic   **a.** felt sure, certain
2. convinced   **b.** lack of feeling or respect
3. fragile   **c.** keeps food cool and fresh
4. insensitivity   **d.** preventing infection
5. refrigerator   **e.** delicate, easily broken

 Imagine Ernie is writing a letter to his cousin, Charlie, telling him about Bigfoot.

Write the letter and say what each member of the family, including Ernie, wants to do.

71

The Apostrophe – Possessive Nouns

- A possessive noun indicates ownership. When two nouns meet and the first one 'owns' the second, then the first noun is known as the possessive noun. It takes the apostrophe.

  a) Singular owners: the dancer's shoes, the child's mother, but Charles' coat.

  b) Plural owners: the dancers' shoes (more than one dancer), the drivers' cars (more than one driver), but the children's mother.

 Rewrite these sentences. Mark in the apostrophe only where necessary. The first one is done for you.

1. The detectives found a doctor's telescope and some nurses' uniforms.
2. My fathers father is my grandfather.
3. The suns rays almost blinded the tourists.
4. The teachers cars are parked at the front of the school.
5. We decided to raise money for a childrens hospital.
6. Our neighbours garden is beautifully landscaped.
7. The factories waste materials caused the death of the fish.
8. The students discovered that the towns population rose after the war.
9. The deers enclosure had a high fence around it.
10. When Cathys camera fell, she burst into tears.

 Write the following in shorter form, using an apostrophe. Then put each phrase into a sentence.

1. the nests of the crows
2. the parrot belonging to Susan
3. the tail belonging to our dog
4. the streets of the cities
5. the weapons of the cavemen
6. the shops belonging to the Springers
7. the boots belonging to the player
8. the lambs of the sheep

 Write the following, inserting apostrophes where necessary.

In the police station a row was brewing over who owned the diamonds. Mr Roberts was certain they were his wifes. His sister-in-law said they were hers. The detective in charge announced that until they could decide they were the stations diamonds.

Using a Dictionary

● A dictionary may be used:
   a. to find the correct meaning of a word,
   b. to check the correct spelling of a word,
   c. to check whether a word is a noun, an adjective, a verb or an adverb.

 Arrange each group of letters below in alphabetical order. Look at the second, third, even fourth letters, if necessary.

A	B	C	D
proof	lopsided	grant	knowing
parsley	loyal	gracious	journey
produce	locality	grade	jubilee
photograph	loose	greed	knowledge
publicity	loophole	grammar	jubilant
possess	longitude	gram	kidney

B **Use your dictionary to check if the following words are nouns, adjectives, verbs or adverbs.**

nephew	negotiate	glorious	receptionist	electric	suddenly
translate	imprison	finally	comfortable	population	volunteer

C **Read the definitions of the words in the box below.**

Rewrite the sentences below. Choose the correct word for the spaces and in brackets write the number of the meaning that applies to it.

apply (v)	**1.** To put on.	dull (adj)	**1.** Not sharp.
	2. To ask for a job.		**2.** Boring.
date (n)	**1.** The day, month and year.	film (n)	**1.** A moving picture.
	2. An arrangement to meet.		**2.** A thin coating.

1. The book I'm reading at the moment is very dull (2).
2. I had to _____ ( ) a lot of paint.
3. There was a _____ ( ) of dust on the furniture.
4. Don't forget that we have a _____ ( ) to go to the cinema.
5. When I hit my head, I felt a _____ ( ) pain.
6. Peter intends to _____ ( ) for the post of gardener.
7. Write the _____ ( ) under the address.

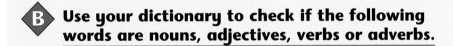

Changing Words

- When we use words a lot we sometimes shorten them by leaving letters out. Did you know that **bus** was once **omnibus**?

 Write down the longer words for these.

plane   phone   bike   fridge   pub   exam

 Write down the shorter words for these. (If you are unsure, check their meanings in a dictionary.)

microphone   laboratory   fanatic

- Quite often the word **of** became shortened to **o'**. The **f** was replaced by an apostrophe **'**. Other words have become shortened too.

 Work out what these are.

o'clock   Hallowe'en   fish 'n' chips

- We also form new words from the first letters of words or phrases.
  CD means compact disc.
  Radar was once a code-word from **ra**dio **d**etecting **a**nd **r**anging.

D **Find out what these mean.**

SW   NE   PS   a.s.a.p.   CD-ROM   e.g.

- Sometimes we drop whole words or combine words:
  transistor is *transfer + resistor*

E **Write down the words we use for these.**

moving picture   zoological gardens   smoke + fog   camera + recorder

F **Now think of five first names that have been shortened, like this.**

Liz (Elizabeth)

Dropping and Keeping e

● When a word ends in **e** and you want to add **ing**, you must drop the **e** like this: take + ing = taking.

 Correct these sentences.

1. Kevin was hopeing that the football manager would select him.
2. Dilly was makeing a clay monster with wobbly eyes.
3. They were now liveing in a caravan near the beach.
4. I have such a likeing for strawberries, ice-cream and chocolate sauce!
5. Marie loved the danceing class, but Kate never looked forward to it.

 You need to drop the e when you add other endings beginning with a vowel.

joke + **ing** = **joking**   joke + **ed** = **joked**   joke + **er** = **joker**

Follow the rule and then copy and complete the table.

	ing	ed	er	en	y	ous	age
taste	tasting	tasted	taster		tasty		
wipe							
use							
fame							
shake							
noise							

Remember these common exceptions!   ageing   mileage

When a word ends in e and you want to add an ending that begins with a consonant, keep the e, like this.
hope + ful = hopeful.

 Add ful or ly to these words.

love   care   force   tune   lone   late   spite   bare   grave

Midwinter Day

Will lives with his family who are farmers. It is the morning of his birthday, three days before Christmas. The sky has been full of snow which has refused to fall. The animals have been uneasy and there have been strange occurrences.

"Robin!" he said loudly. "Wake up!" But Robin breathed slowly and rhythmically as before and did not stir.

He ran into the bedroom next door, the familiar small room that he had once shared with James, and shook James roughly by the shoulder. But when the shaking was done, James lay motionless, deeply asleep.

Will went out on to the landing again and took a long breath, and he shouted with all his might: "Wake up! Wake up, everyone!"

He did not now expect any response, and none came. There was a total silence, as deep and timeless as the blanketing snow; the house and everyone in it lay in a sleep that would not be broken.

Will went downstairs to pull on his boots and the old sheepskin jacket that had belonged, before him, to two or three of his brothers in turn. Then he went out of the back door, closing it quietly behind him, and stood looking out through the quick white vapour of his breath.

The strange white world lay stroked by silence. No birds sang. The garden was no longer there, in this forested land. Nor were the outbuildings nor the old crumbling walls. There lay only a narrow clearing round the house now, hummocked with unbroken snowdrifts, before the trees began, with a narrow path leading away. Will set out down the white tunnel of the path slowly, stepping high to keep the snow out of his boots. As soon as he moved away from the house he felt very much alone, and he made himself go on without looking back over his shoulder, because he knew that when he looked, he would find that the house was gone.

He accepted everything that came into his mind, without thought or question, as if he was moving through a dream. But a deeper part of him knew that he was not dreaming. He was crystal-clear awake, in a Midwinter Day that had been waiting for him to wake into it since the day he had been born, and, he somehow knew, for centuries before that. Tomorrow will be beyond imagining ... Will came out of the white-arched path into the road, paved smooth with snow and edged everywhere by the great trees, and he looked up between the branches and saw a single black rook flap slowly past, high in the early sky.

From *The Dark Is Rising* by Susan Cooper

Answer these questions.

1. Explain what has happened to Robin and James. What do you think could have caused it?
2. What has happened to the birds?
3. Explain 'The garden was no longer there, in this forested land'.
4. Why does Will not look back?
5. What do you think could have caused the strange happenings?
6. Why do you think Will has not been affected? (Read the last paragraph again.)
7. What else is unaffected besides Will? Do you think this is a good or bad sign?
8. What does 'Tomorrow will be beyond imagining ...' mean?
9. Some parts of the story seem real and some seem to be fantasy. Write down an example of each.

 Imagery.

Writers create pictures in the mind to make their words come alive. We call these **images**. They can appeal to different senses such as sound, taste and smell, as well as sight.

1. Think about what the passage is about and explain why these two images fit into it:

   quick white vapour of his breath   crystal-clear awake

2. Sometimes writers compare one thing with another to make an image. They use the words 'like' or 'as'. We call this a **simile**.

   Example: 'as deep and timeless as the blanketing snow'

3. Write similes for the following:
   a. The leafless trees were like _____ .
   b. It was as grey and lifeless as _____ .
   c. The curved snowdrift was like _____ .

Prepositions

- Look at these sentences. **(i)** The stranger walked towards the door. **(ii)** The stranger stood near the door. **(iii)** The stranger knocked on the door.
- The relationship between 'stranger' and 'door' is shown by the words **towards**, **near** and **on**. They, and words like them, are called **prepositions**.

 Write the sentences and ring the prepositions.

1. It was raining so we sheltered under the tree.
2. The mouse ran into the hole.
3. There were sunny spells between the showers.
4. She fell off her bicycle.
5. The dog leapt over the wall.

 Write the following sentences. Fill in the blanks with prepositions.

1. The river flows _____ a toll bridge.
2. The waves lashed _____ the cliffs.
3. We live _____ a forest which is _____ a motorway.
4. The bus stopped _____ the railway station.
5. Visitors came _____ foreign countries _____ the museum.

C **Explain in your own words the difference between each pair of sentences.**

1. The children are *in* bed.
   The children climbed *into* bed.
2. Sam went *back* to the house.
   Sam went *up* to the house.
3. We went *through* the house to get to the garden.
   We went *into* the house to get to the garden.
4. Sam and Catherine went to the cinema *before* the restaurant.
   Sam and Catherine went to the cinema *behind* the restaurant.
5. The police officer drove *by* the station.
   The police officer drove *into* the station.
6. We sat *under* a tree to eat our picnic.
   We sat *next to* a tree to eat our picnic.

Interviews

- A good interviewer asks searching questions. These are questions which persuade the interviewee (the person being interviewed) to answer in sentences, describing his/her thoughts in detail. Try to avoid asking questions which can be answered with a simple "Yes" or "No".

 A   <u>**Make up your own questions.**</u>

Imagine you met an historical character such as Florence Nightingale, Christopher Columbus, Joan of Arc, Harry Houdini or whoever you prefer. You get the once-in-a-lifetime opportunity to interview this famous person about his/her life. Think about the questions you should ask. Here are some examples. Copy the sentences and complete them in your own way.

What was it like growing up in ...?

Did you always want to ...?

Where did you start ...?

Who influenced you ...?

Why did ...?

How did you feel ...?

Can you remember when ...?

What was your favourite ...?

What do you remember most about ...?

Are you surprised by ...?

How do you feel now about ..?

What message ...?

 B   <u>**Be a reporter.**</u>

A reporter must ask specific questions about an event, so that he/she can 'paint a picture' of what happened, in an article. Look at this scene of an accident. What questions would you ask if you were assigned to the job of reporting on it? Write the conversations you had with the witnesses. Then write a short article reporting what happened and what you think should be done to prevent future accidents.

A–Z Factfile

 Produce an A–Z factfile on a subject of your choice.

Pick a wide-ranging subject such as the Olympic Games, the World Cup, Music, Television Programmes, Food or Famous People. Each letter of the alphabet is used to begin a statement connected to the subject. You can draw a picture for each entry.

Example: Subject title – The Olympic Games.

> **A is for** Athens, where the Games were revived in 1896 by the Frenchman, Baron Pierre de Coubertin. He stated, 'The important thing is not winning but taking part'.
>
> **B is for** ...

What Happened Next?

 Describe what happened in the first two scenes.
Then write and draw your own concluding scene.
What do you imagine the driver saw ahead of him?

Cleaning Up

1. Fact/interpretation.

- State five facts (things that are true) about this picture.
- Then suggest three things that you might interpret (what might be true) from it.

2. Observation.

- Are all the children dressed in the same way? Explain.
- What are they doing?
- What are they wearing on their hands and over their tops? Why?

3. Tell a story.

Tell a short story, choosing one of these beginnings to get you started:

- They all said my idea wouldn't work, but ...
- It wasn't easy getting up at 6 o'clock ...
- I was in the park when I saw ...

4. Thought provokers.

- What is the boy in the background doing? Is he part of the group?
- Why are the children doing all this?
- Where are they?
- Are you a member of any group? Talk about it.
- Have you ever done something like this?

Where Eagles Dare

In Where Eagles Dare, *seven men enter the Schloss Adler, the castle of the eagle, and free an imprisoned man.*

With deadly determination Smith and Schaffer gripped the great steel bolt that connected the car to the moving cable. There was nothing else to hold on to. The roof was solidly coated with ice and they could find no foot-hold. Their bodies slipped uncontrollably in all directions with the violent swinging of the car beneath them. The pull on hands and arms and shoulders was even worse than Smith had feared: and the worst was yet to come.

The cable car was past the last support post now. Soon the moment of truth. A minute from then, Smith thought, and they could both be lying broken and lifeless on the rocks over seventy metres below. On the last stage of its climb, the cable car seemed to be rising straight up into the air. The castle walls, with the cable-station at the base, were almost directly above their heads.

"Oh, my God!" Schaffer groaned. "Look at the slope of that roof!"

The front of the car passed under the edge of the station roof. A moment later Smith sprang forward and upwards, throwing himself bodily on to the roof. His right arm struck downwards and the knife blade stuck firmly in the wood below the coating of ice. Less than a second later Schaffer had landed beside him, his knife striking the roof at exactly the same moment as his body.

The blade broke. Schaffer opened his hand, dropped the handle and snatched in despair at the ice. He dug both hands in with all the strength that was in him, and he slowed, but not enough. His toes failed to find any hold and he knew he was slipping out over the edge.

Smith's jump had knocked the breath out of him. Several seconds passed before he realised that Schaffer was not lying on the roof beside him. As he turned round, he sensed rather than saw the despair in Schaffer's white face. With a speed and power that would have been impossible a few seconds earlier, he brought his left hand flashing down. Schaffer cried out in pain as the grip of steel closed over his right wrist.

For some seconds they lay like that, the lives of both depending on the small blade of Smith's knife. Then Schaffer felt the shaking of Smith's left arm and began to pull himself slowly upwards.

Alistair Maclean (Abridged by Norah Woolard)

82

A **Answer these questions.**

1. Where was the cable car taking Smith and Schaffer?
2. Why do you think they travelled on its roof?
3. What dangerous task faced them as they approached their destination?
4. What was the station roof made of?
5. Why didn't Smith catch Schaffer's arm a few seconds earlier?
6. Why did both lives depend on Smith's small blade?
7. Which man was stronger? Why do you think so?
8. Do you think Schaffer fell off the roof? What happened next?
9. In what kind of area did this scene occur? How do you know?
10. Has anybody ever saved you from being hurt? How did it happen?

B **Each numbered sentence tells us something that happened (the effect). In each group, write the lettered sentence that tells why or gives a reason (the cause).**

1. Schaffer and Smith slipped uncontrollably *because*
   a. they were drunk.
   b. they weren't used to riding on cable cars.
   c. the car swung wildly and they couldn't stand on the iced roof.
2. The blade broke *because*
   a. it was too old and rusty.
   b. Schaffer mistimed the striking action with his knife.
   c. Schaffer struck it against stone.
3. Schaffer dropped the handle *because*
   a. it was hurting him.
   b. he needed to free his hand and prevent himself from falling.
   c. it slipped out of his hand.

C **Find the words in the passage which mean the same as the clues below.**

1. Mind firmly made up, fixed purpose
2. Dead
3. With no hope
4. Joined or linked together
5. Relying on
6. Grabbed or seized suddenly

D **Use your imagination.**

How would you and a team of agents break into a heavily fortified castle? Would you parachute in or trick the security staff? Describe your successful mission.

Dahn the Plug'ole

A muvver was barfin' 'er biby one night,
The youngest of ten and a tiny young mite,
The muvver was pore and the biby was thin,
Only a skelington covered in skin;
The muvver turned rahnd for the soap orf the rack,
She was but a moment, but when she turned back,
The biby was gorn; and in anguish she cried,
"Oh, where is my biby?" — the Angels
replied:
"Your biby 'as fell dahn the plug'ole,
Your biby 'as gorn dahn the plug;
The poor little thing was so skinny and thin
'E oughter been barfed in a jug;
Your biby is perfectly 'appy,
'E won't need a barf any more,
Your biby 'as fell dahn the plug'ole,
Not lorst, but gorn before!"

Anon

 Answer these questions.

1. Write down what the following words mean: 'dahn', 'plug'ole', 'muvver', 'barfin', 'biby', 'pore', 'rahnd', 'orf', 'gorn', 'lorst'.

2. What happened to the baby?

3. Why should the baby have been bathed in a jug?

4. Why did the angels tell the mother not to worry? Explain what the last line means.

5. Do you think the story is true? Say why or why not.

6. What dialect (style of language) do you think the poem is written in?

7. How do the words help you read the poem in the right way?

8. Who wrote the poem?

 Find other poems in the library which are written in dialect. (They are often written by Anon.)

Try writing your own dialect poem about school or friendship. Redraft it and present it to others.

Timber!

1. Fact/interpretation.
- State five facts (things that are true) that are obvious in this picture.
- Then suggest three things that you might interpret (which might be true) from it.

2. Observation.
- What kind of trees are in the picture? Roughly how tall are they?
- Describe what the machine is doing to the trees. How else could this be done?
- How does the machine operator ensure his/her safety? Is the work neatly executed?

3. Tell a story.
Tell a short story, choosing one of these beginnings to get you started.
- I was just standing there minding my own business when ...
- For one terrifying moment, I thought ...
- They shouldn't be allowed ...

4. Thought provokers.
- Why do you think they are clearing these trees?
- What will be put there instead?
- Explain why the lower section of the trees is so brown, with no vegetation.
- Do you agree with the chopping down of trees for the sake of development? What can you do?

The y Rule

- When a word ends in **y** with a consonant before it, change the **y** to **ie** when you add a suffix:

  shy   shies   shied

  The horse shies in front of that jump, every time!

 Change these words in the same way and write them out adding s **and** ed.

fry   cry   spy   try   dry

- But remember, when we add the suffixes ly and ing to such words we simply add the suffix like this:

  shy   shyly   shying

 There are spelling mistakes in some of these sentences. Decide which ones and write them out correctly.

1. The pot-bellied pigs were thrilled with their warm and comfortable new stys.
2. He accepted the present shiely and walked away with embarrassment.
3. Blue skies, sun, sea and sand were all the children wanted on holiday.
4. She was not pleased when she discovered that Martin had been prieing into her business affairs.
5. Harry had a clever sense of humour and always told his jokes dryly.
6. Wendy relys on Mandy to help her get the children to school.
7. They lived on a small island off the west coast and all their goods were supplied by the mainland ferrys.
8. Sue spent hours copieing out the notices for the exhibition and secretly Dina thought it was a waste of time.

 Write out this passage, correcting the mistakes.

Karen watched the birds flying overhead as she took in her washing, dryed by the sunshine. She took a closer look at her shirt and noticed that the dryed-in stain from last night was still there. She could have cried, but she didn't. She just tryed not to think how expensive it had been, as she walked into the house.

Proof-reading

 A **Correct the punctuation in the following.**
(There may be more than one sentence in each.)

1. my mum shouted Take off those filthy trainers just look at what theyre doing to the carpet

2. cathy who is my best friend has green spiky hair She looks really tough but shes always kind to me

3. Im very fussy about what i eat in my sandwiches i only like cheese peanut butter banana and marmite sometimes my dad forgets and gives me ham or egg so i swap them with peters

4. the tiny teacher told us in her loud booming voice that we must have our homework finished by friday i whispered to tom i bet nicky has finished hers already we could copy it unfortunately i didnt whisper quietly enough and now i have a detention on friday as well

 B **Proof-read this letter by copying it and underlining the words that should have capital letters or that are not spelled correctly. Insert the correct punctuation marks at the end of every sentence.**

Chilly House
Freezer Street
Narnia
Christmas Eve

Dear King Aslan

How are you on this last saturday before christmas are the earthlings still with you Give them my fondest regardes when you sea them where would narnia be without them espeshially the youngest one lucy I suppose she's queen lucy now, the little retch.

I'm sure you don't beleeve that i've gone to all this trouble of writing to wish you a happie christmas Well you're write, i haven't do you imagin i'm going soft in my old age Not me my frend, Aslan I want you all to no that i intende regaining the thrown at cair Paravel in the new year I've been reading 'gone with the wind' and I promise you that I too, will return in plain english, that means you shood get out of town now

don't say I didn't warn you See you next year.

yours sincerly

The White Which

Prefixes – Spellings and Meanings

Sometimes we can work out the meaning of words if we understand the meaning of the prefix.

in, **im**, **ir** and **il** mean **not**

 Read these sentences and write down what you think the words in bold mean.

1. When he turned his head and saw the giant striding towards the children he thought he had never seen such an **incredible** sight.

2. As they examined the photograph carefully, they saw a small **inconspicuous** figure in the background which gave them a vital clue.

3. He recounted the story in a cold, **impersonal** manner and Trudy was not convinced she was hearing the truth.

4. Her games, toys and CDs were organised in such an **impeccable** manner that Desmond thought they must be very important to her.

5. "This is most **irregular**!" snapped the little man at the children. "I'm afraid I can't allow you to enter unless you fill in this form."

6. "My computer has performed an **illegal** task! Will I get punished?" wailed Jerry.

7. "Your handwriting is completely **illegible**, Mary, I can't read a word of it," said Sonia.

8. It is completely **impractical** to go walking in the mountains without your walking boots.

9. "I'm sure they gave me **inaccurate** data on the earthquake," sighed the scientist. "It really doesn't add up."

10. "The speaker is completely **inarticulate**, I really don't know what he's talking about," moaned Mrs Andrews.

11. Simon and Lucy agreed that they were **incompatible**. They could not agree on anything.

12. It's a shame that my language skills are **irrelevant** to my new job.

13. Matthew was convinced that his new teacher was **infallible**.

14. It was Sally's fault that she had **indigestion** because she had eaten too quickly.

 Find five more words in a dictionary, each beginning with in, im, ir and il. Write a question to show their meanings, like this.

Is Neil always so **impatient** and bad-tempered with Annie if he has to wait for her?

Air Disaster

1. Fact/interpretation.

- State five facts (things that are true) about this picture.
- Then suggest three things that you might interpret (which might be true) from it.

2. Observation.

- Is there any indication of the name and size of this plane? Where did it crash?
- What was the red vehicle used for? Who are the people in the photograph?
- What time of year was it? Describe the weather.

3. Tell/dramatise a story.

Tell a short story, using one of these beginnings to get you started. Tape record your answers.

- We heard a deafening crash and were horrified ...
- "I was so lucky," said ...
- I thought I heard a voice moaning beneath ...

4. Thought provokers.

- Was this photograph taken immediately after the crash? Why do you think so?
- Do you think that there were survivors? What would you do in an emergency crash landing?
- What might have caused this crash? Do you think aeroplanes are safe?

A Wanderer's Song

A wind's in the heart of me, a fire's in my heels.
I am tired of brick and stone and rumbling wagon-wheels;
I hunger for the sea's edge, the limits of the land
Where the wild old Atlantic is shouting on the sand.

Oh I'll be going, leaving the noises of the street.
To where a lifting foresail-foot is yanking at the sheet;
To a windy, tossing anchorage where yawls and ketches ride,
Oh, I'll be going, going, until I meet the tide.

And first I'll hear the sea-wind, the mewing of the gulls,
The clucking, sucking of the sea about the rusty hulls.
The songs at the capstan in the hooker warping out.
And then the heart of me'll know I'm there or thereabout.

Oh I am tired of brick and stone, the heart of me is sick,
For windy green, unquiet sea, the realm of Moby Dick;
And I'll be going, going, from the roaring of the wheels,
For a wind's in the heart of me, a fire's in my heels.

John Masefield

A **Answer these questions.**

1. Why is the poem titled 'A Wanderer's Song'?
2. What kind of area does the poet live in?
3. In your own words, describe what he's tired of.
4. Was the poem written recently? How do you know?
5. Where does he want to be and what attracts him to it?
6. Find out what 'Moby Dick' means.
7. Write five adjectives that describe how the poet feels now.
8. Do you like where you live? Why? If you had a 'fire in your heels', where would you like to go?

B **Sometimes people who have a wandering personality are described as being 'up in the clouds'.**

Use your senses and write a poem about floating on a cloud. What do you see?
Begin each verse with the words 'From my cloud ...'
Example: 'From my cloud, I see a wet road, glistening like silver, shining like gold.'

Many Languages

There are a large number of English words which come from other languages.

 Do you know where these words come from?
Try to guess by writing them underneath these headings.

Spanish	Italian	Chinese	Indian	Arabic

polo   yoga   wok   spaghetti   siesta   sofa

paparazzi   graffiti   tomato   broccoli   algebra

veranda   tango   sherbet   bungalow

chop suey   macaroni   tea   zero   lemon

cot   curry   kung fu

Work with a friend. Check in an etymology dictionary any words you are uncertain of.

 Many of these words are easy to remember
because they are spelled as they sound.

   1. Choose ten words and split them into their syllables, like this:
   veranda   ve-ran-da
   2. Underline all those words that end in **i**. Remember, that in words like these, **i** sounds like **ee**.

 Can you think of any more words that come from other languages?

Write them down and then check their origins.

Donkey Rides

1. Fact/interpretation.

- State five facts (things that are true) about this picture.
- Then suggest three things that you might interpret (which might be true) from it.

2. Observation.

- What 'services' do the characters offer? What is attached to the sign?
- Where did the number plate come from? Was it always attached to the cart?
- What's unusual about the dog? Why might the donkey have difficulty in seeing it?

3. Tell a story.

Tell a short story, choosing one of these beginnings to get you started.

- My grandad always says that everyone needs a friend ...
- We left the souvenir shop and when we turned the corner ...
- If he expects me to stay ...

4. Thought provokers.

- Why do people spend money on 'services' like this? Would you?
- What other tricks might the animals have been trained to do?
- Why are the windows of the building fogged up? Is it derelict?

In for the High Jump

1. Fact/interpretation.

- State five facts (things that are true) about this picture.
- Then suggest three things that you might interpret (which might be true) from it.

2. Observation.

- What event is this?
- What other 'jumping' events are there?
- Do you think she will do the jump successfully? Why?

3. Tell a story.

Tell a short story, choosing one of these beginnings to get you started.

- I had trained all year for ...
- Suddenly I felt ...
- They said I couldn't do it ...

4. Thought provokers.

- Who do you think she is competing for – herself, her club or her country?
- Why do some people prefer 'individual sports' and others prefer 'team sports'?
- What sport do you prefer? Would you like to be a player or an official?

The i, e and c Rule

● Do you know this spelling rhyme?

i before **e** except after **c**,
when the sound is **ee**.

● Apply the rule and compare these words:
believe   receive

 Complete these sentences by writing out the unfinished word correctly.

1. Caroline took a huge handker_____ from her pocket and blew her nose.
2. Tarik sighed with rel_____ as the old car rumbled up the drive.
3. "Now, don't get up to mis_____ in that sand-pit!" yelled Michael's mum.
4. He carefully hung the new light from the c_____ing and almost immediately it fell down.
5. Uncle Graham was a generous man who always treated his nephew and n_____ to a day out.
6. Dougie was given a re_____ for the money and was told to collect the CD in the afternoon.
7. The boy was constantly boasting about his computer and Kisha thought he was very con_____ .
8. Gary watched the lion open its mouth slowly and roar so f_____ that he thought the animal must be in pain.
9. "Would you like an extra p_____ of my apple and blackberry pie?" said Gran cheerfully.
10. The pathway was shrouded in mist, but Janie could just per_____ a small cottage in the distance.

 Write out the paragraph and correct the mistakes.

Paula drummed her fingers and stared at the cieling. She couldn't believe how much their cheif went on. After all, they were only a small gang. Natalie was excited though; she had recieved some news about the boys' gang. Her peircing voice droned on. Paula sighed and prayed that she would try to be brief.

Remember these exceptions: science   seize   weird   protein
Keep a note of any other exceptions you find.

94

Write a Letter

- Do you remember how to write a letter?
- Look through some magazines and newspapers until you find an article or a photograph that 'catches your eye'. You might pick an article/photograph that reminds you of something that you really enjoyed, that angers you, that you agree with, that you have an alternative opinion about, and so on.
- Write a letter to the editor of the magazine/newspaper, giving your opinion.

Questionnaires

You may be stopped in the street sometime by somebody who wants you to complete a questionnaire. Usually most of the questions can be answered quickly by just ticking a box. As a result, only certain choices are offered for these questions. Look at the questions on the form below. What would your answers be? Now make up your own questionnaire for a friend to complete.

1. Boy ☐   Girl ☐

2. Age: 6–9 ☐ 10–12 ☐ 13–15 ☐

3. Hours of TV watched per week
Less than 5 ☐
5 to 10 ☐
11 to 20 ☐
21 to 30 ☐
more than 30 ☐

4. Favourite type of TV programme
Music ☐
Sport ☐
Comedy ☐
Films ☐
Soaps ☐
Other ☐

5. Favourite food
Chocolate ☐
Fruit ☐
Vegetables ☐
Chips ☐
Burgers ☐
Other ☐

6. Household chores
Which one do you least like?
Washing or drying dishes ☐
Tidying rooms ☐
Doing errands ☐
Baby-sitting ☐
Gardening ☐

7. School year
Which of the following would you like?
Longer Christmas/Summer holidays ☐
One week's break, every six weeks ☐
Longer school day, with more holidays ☐
Shorter school day, with fewer holidays ☐
School year left as it is ☐

8. World leader
If you were a world leader, which issue would concern you most?
Establishing world peace ☐
Creating full employment ☐
Tackling crime ☐
Solving famine problems ☐
Ensuring equal rights for all ☐

Thank you for your co-operation.

Sitting Around

1. Fact/interpretation.

- State five facts (things that are true) about this picture.
- Then suggest three things that you might interpret (which might be true) from it.

2. Observation.

- What season is it? What evidence supports your view?
- Describe what each person is wearing.
- What indicates that the steps don't lead immediately onto a beach?

3. Tell a story.

Tell a short story, choosing one of these beginnings to get you started.

- As I sat there, I remembered ...
- I'm never talking to my sister again ...
- Jayne wondered if her mum ...

4. Thought provokers.

- How do these people get on together?
- Do you like being with your family? Where?
- Why are they sitting on the steps? What do you think they are looking at?
- What do the steps lead up to? Why are railings needed?